THE CIVIL LAW TRADITION

JOHN HENRY MERRYMAN AND
ROGELIO PÉREZ-PERDOMO

The Civil Law Tradition

AN INTRODUCTION TO THE LEGAL SYSTEMS OF
EUROPE AND LATIN AMERICA

Fourth Edition

STANFORD UNIVERSITY PRESS
STANFORD, CALIFORNIA

Stanford University Press
Stanford, California

Printed in the United States of America
on acid-free, archival-quality paper

Library of Congress Cataloging-in-Publication Data

Names: Merryman, John Henry, author. |
Pérez-Perdomo, Rogelio, author.
Title: The civil law tradition : an introduction to the
legal systems of Europe and Latin America /
John Henry Merryman and Rogelio Pérez-Perdomo.
Description: Fourth edition. | Stanford, California :
Stanford University Press, [2018] | Includes bibliographical
references and index.
Identifiers: LCCN 2018012684 (print) | LCCN 2018013709
(e-book) | ISBN 9781503607552 (e-book) |
ISBN 9781503606814 (cloth : alk. paper) |
ISBN 9781503607545 (pbk. : alk. paper) |
ISBN 9781503607552 (e-book)
Subjects: LCSH: Civil law systems.
Classification: LCC K585 (e-book) | LCC K585 .M467 2018
(print) | DDC 340.5/6—dc23
LC record available at https://lccn.loc.gov/2018012684

Typeset by Newgen in 10/12 Galliard

For Nancy, Len, Sam, and Bruce,
in celebration of April 1, 1953,
and other great days.
—J.H.M.

For Camila.
—R.P.P.

CONTENTS

PREFACE TO THE FOURTH EDITION

PROFESSOR JOHN HENRY MERRYMAN passed away on August 3, 2015, after a long, active, and productive life. He made enormous contributions to legal scholarship: he created a new field, art in the law, and he conceived a new approach to comparative law. He was interested in comparing legal systems in action and using the social sciences and quantitative indicators in his analysis. He studied the Italian law in depth and was familiar with French and German law as well the main Latin American legal systems.

This book is one of his early works in comparative law. It is a masterpiece: clear, comprehensive, and at the same time of an unusual depth. The previous three editions in English are a good proof of its acceptance in the English-speaking (common law) world. The translation into many languages of the countries of the civil law tradition shows its worldwide acceptance. Professor Merryman asked me to participate in its updating for the third edition in 2006, and I was honored when he recognized me as his coauthor. In 2013 and 2014 we taught together Comparative Law and Society at Stanford Law School, and this was the occasion for new conversations on the continuing evolution of the civil law tradition. Generally, we agreed in our understanding of these changes. I think this fourth edition reflects these conversations and our areas of agreement.

In the first two editions, it was clear that an American jurist was explaining the civil law tradition in comparison with his native tradition. I am a native of the civil law tradition, but in this edition the American law is maintained as an anchor for the comparative law purposes. The general appreciation and success of the previous editions of this book encouraged a conservative approach that avoided unnecessary changes.

Stanford, 2018   R.P.P.

PREFACE TO THE ORIGINAL EDITION

THIS BOOK is written for amateurs, not professionals. It speaks to the general reader who wants to know what it is that binds together the legal systems of Western Europe and Latin America and that distinguishes them from the legal systems of the Anglo-American world; to the nonlawyer who wishes to know something about the legal side of European and Latin American culture; to the student seeking collateral reading for a course in history, politics, sociology, philosophy, international relations, area studies, or law. This book may also have some use among lawyers who have not studied foreign and comparative law and wish, for practical or other reasons, to begin to remedy this deficiency. It can provide background reading for persons with public or private business in Europe or Latin America (or other civil law nations). My professional colleagues in foreign and comparative law, however, are likely to find the work too elementary and too general to engage their interest.

Although I have tried to make it clear in the text that this book does not attempt to describe any specific national legal system, a special word should be said here about the peculiar problem posed by France and Germany. Each of these nations has made a major contribution to the civil law tradition, and each still occupies a position of intellectual leadership in the civil law world. At the same time, neither is a "typical" civil law system. Indeed, they are in a sense the least typical of all. The French revolutionary ideology and the French style of codification had only a limited impact on German law. German legal science has never really caught on in France. Elsewhere in the civil law world, however, there has been a strong tendency to receive and fuse both influences. This is particularly true in Mediterranean Europe and Latin America, but it also applies to some extent to most other parts of the civil law world. French or German readers may find much in this book that is not representative of their legal system. The reason is that their system is atypical. The civil law world includes a great number of national legal systems in Europe, Latin America, Asia, Africa, and the Middle East. This book is about the legal tradition they share, not about French or German law.

Something should also be said about perspective. I do not mean to suggest that all lawyers in civil law nations accept and believe in those aspects of their tradition that will appear to the reader to be excessive or deficient. On the contrary, I have tried to indicate throughout (and to hammer the point home again in Chapter XIX, which I beg the reader not to skip) that I am describing "prevailing" attitudes. There is the common run of lawyers, and there is the sophisticated, critical jurist at the growing point of legal thought. Sophisticated jurists always constitute the smaller and less representative group, but even in the most backward nation one can expect to find a few lawyers who will honestly say: "I don't think that way at all." In a more advanced civil law nation like France or Germany, the proportion of enlightened and liberated lawyers and the extent to which the legal order has freed itself of the defects of the tradition will be greater. That is another indication of the atypicality of France and Germany. This book, however, is about the way the common run of lawyers in the civil law world generally think, even though the avant-garde of legal thought tells them they are wrong.

Dean Bayless A. Manning of the Stanford School of Law persuaded me that there was a need for this book, and encouraged me to write it. Three outstanding comparative lawyers—Professors Mauro Cappelletti of the University of Florence, F. H. Lawson, formerly of Oxford University, and Konrad Zweigert, of the Max Planck Institute in Hamburg—kindly read the manuscript and suggested a number of changes that improved it. One of my colleagues at Stanford, Dr. George Torzsay-Biber, was particularly helpful on a number of questions concerning Roman civil law. Generations of imaginative and industrious scholars have produced a rich literature on foreign and comparative law, from which most of the ideas contained in this book were drawn. Dr. Hein Kötz, Research Associate at the Max Planck Institute in Hamburg, and Gernot Reiners, a Teaching Fellow at the Stanford School of Law, 1967–68, assisted me in a variety of ways, and in particular gave me authoritative information on German law. Mrs. Lois St. John Rigg prepared the manuscript for publication with skill, patience, and good humor. To all, my thanks.

Stanford, 1969   J.H.M.

THE CIVIL LAW TRADITION

I

TWO LEGAL TRADITIONS

THERE ARE two highly influential legal traditions in the contemporary world: civil law and common law. This book is about the older, more widely distributed, and more influential of them: the civil law tradition.

The reader will observe that the term used is "legal tradition," not "legal system." The purpose is to distinguish between two quite different ideas. A legal system, as that term is here used, is an operating set of legal institutions, procedures, and rules. In this sense, there are one federal and fifty state legal systems in the United States, separate legal systems in each of the other nations, and still other distinct legal systems in such organizations as the European Union and the United Nations. In a world organized into sovereign states and organizations of states, there are as many legal systems as there are such states and organizations.

National legal systems are frequently classified into groups or families. Thus, the legal systems of England, New Zealand, California, and New York are called "common law" systems, and there are good reasons to group them together in this way. But it is inaccurate to suggest that they have identical legal institutions, processes, and rules. On the contrary, there is great diversity among them, not only in their substantive rules of law but also in their institutions and processes.

Similarly, France, Germany, Italy, and Switzerland have their own legal systems, as do Argentina, Brazil, and Chile. It is true that they are all frequently spoken of as "civil law" nations, and we try in this book to explain why it makes sense to group them together in this way. But it is important to recognize that there are great differences between the operating legal systems in these countries. They have quite different legal rules, legal procedures, and legal institutions.

In former editions of this book a third major legal tradition was briefly recognized. For much of the twentieth century, socialist law reigned in the Soviet Empire, China, and several other nations that embraced state socialism. At that time, even in the official language

1

of diplomats a sharp distinction was made between the first (capitalist) world, the second (socialist) world, and the third (developing) world. Socialist law embraced the political and economic premises and objectives of state socialism, implying a distinctly different vision of the state, law, and society. Indeed, during the height of Soviet state socialism there was an organized effort to construct an independent and valid socialist legal tradition. However, most of the nations with socialist law had previously been participants in the civil law tradition, to which they reverted when the socialist law superstructure collapsed.

Such differences in legal systems are reflections of the fact that for several centuries the world has been divided into individual states, under intellectual conditions that have emphasized the importance of state sovereignty and encouraged a nationalistic emphasis on national characteristics and traditions. In this sense, there is no such thing as *the* civil law system or *the* common law system. Rather, many different legal systems exist within each of these two groups or families of legal systems. But the fact that different legal systems are grouped together under such a rubric as "civil law," for example, indicates that they have something in common, something that distinguishes them from legal systems classified as "common law." It is this uniquely shared something that is here spoken of as a legal tradition and that makes it possible to speak of the French and German (and many other) legal systems as civil law systems.

A legal tradition, as the term implies, is not a set of rules of law about contracts, corporations, and crimes, although such rules will almost always be in some sense a reflection of that tradition. Rather, it is a set of deeply rooted, historically conditioned attitudes about the nature of law, about the role of law in the society and the polity, about the proper organization and operation of a legal system, and about the way law is or should be made, applied, studied, perfected, and taught. The legal tradition relates the legal system to the culture of which it is a partial expression. It puts the legal system into cultural perspective.

Of the great variety of living legal traditions, the two mentioned above are of particular interest because they are in force in powerful, technologically advanced nations and because they have been exported, with greater or lesser effect, to other parts of the world. Of the two, the civil law tradition is both the older and the more widely distributed. It goes back to Roman law, for which historians use the

2

year 450 BC, the supposed date of publication of the Twelve Tables, as the beginning of Roman law. Historians also highlight that the great development happened in the classical period (100 BC to AD 250), and another great moment was the compilation of the classical jurisconsults' opinions by Emperor Justinian in AD 533. The civil law tradition is today the dominant legal tradition in Europe, all of Latin America, many parts of Asia and Africa, and even a few enclaves in the common law world (Louisiana, Quebec, and Puerto Rico). The civil law was the legal tradition familiar to the European scholar-politicians who were the founders of international law. The basic charters and the continuing legal development and operation of the European Union are the work of people trained in the civil law tradition. It is difficult to overstate the influence of the civil law tradition on the law of specific nations, the law of international organizations, and international law.

We in the common law world are not accustomed to thinking in these terms. Hence, it bears repeating that the civil law tradition is older, more widely distributed, and more influential than the common law tradition. In these senses, at least, it is more important. It should be added that many people believe the civil law to be culturally superior to the common law, which seems to them to be relatively crude and unorganized. The question of superiority is really beside the point. Sophisticated comparative lawyers in both traditions long ago abandoned discussions of relative superiority or inferiority. But it is to the point that many people think that their legal system is superior to ours in the United States. That attitude itself has become part of the civil law tradition.

Hence lawyers from a relatively undeveloped nation may be convinced that their legal system is measurably superior to that of the United States or Canada. Unless they have cultivated the comparative law, they may be inclined to patronize a common lawyer. They will recognize the more advanced economic development or envy the standard of living of the other country, but they will find compensatory comfort in thinking of common lawyers as relatively uncultured people. The mirror attitude is also frequent. There are common lawyers who think their legal system and their legal cultures are clearly superior because the country is wealthier or politically more stable. Failure to take these attitudes of some civil lawyers and common lawyers into account can result in misunderstanding and difficult communication. One of the purposes of this book is to enable a better dialogue between civil and common lawyers.

The date commonly used to mark the beginning of the common law tradition is AD 1066, when the Normans defeated the defending natives at Hastings and conquered England. If we accept that date, the common law tradition is well over nine hundred years old. As a result of the remarkable expansion and development of the British Empire during the age of colonialism and empire, however, the common law was very widely distributed. It is today the legal tradition in force in Great Britain, Ireland, the United States, Canada, Australia, and New Zealand, and it has had substantial influence on the law of many nations in Asia and Africa. The birth of the civil law tradition is foggier. Civil lawyers claim to be the inheritors of Roman law, and the translation of this book into Spanish presents it as the tradition of Roman and canonical law. Spanish, Portuguese, and French colonialism expanded it in the world.

Although Japan and China were not colonized by any European country, by the end of the nineteenth century or the beginning of the twentieth they had imported codes and other instruments of the civil law tradition. That is why many jurists from Japan, Korea, and China think of themselves as part of the civil law world. Still, comparative lawyers recognize a distinct tradition in East Asia, whose cultures emphasize social harmony and respect for social hierarchies. Some observers relate these traits to Confucian thought and suggest the existence of a Confucian legal tradition. Certainly, Japanese law and legal culture are not substantially similar to those in Germany, even if the civil code is practically the same and German law books have an audience in Japan. American public law has a strong influence in Japan and Korea, but no one would suggest that they are common law nations.

The Islamic world has felt a variety of significant legal influences. Early in the twentieth century Turkey imported the Swiss civil code as part of its modernization process. Lebanon and Algeria, colonized by the French, received the French law but later became independent and followed their own paths. Other countries, like Yemen and Saudi Arabia, were less influenced by Western law. In many countries with large Islamic populations, their religion has had a vigorous revival and has produced a renewed emphasis on Islamic legal traditions. Still, much secular law in those nations has its origins in the civil law and common law traditions.

The civil law and common law have not been isolated from each other. As components of a common Western history and culture they have had multiple contacts and reciprocal influences. Common lawyers and civil lawyers coexisted in England for centuries. The constitution of the United States could be partially explained by the influence of the European Enlightenment. Later, United States constitutionalism had an enormous influence in Latin America and Europe. Judicial review, for example, is now firmly embedded in both traditions. The condominium, a civil law invention, has been enthusiastically embraced in the United States, and many civil law systems have incorporated the common law trust. The education of lawyers in universities, perhaps the most distinctive trait of the civil law tradition, is now accepted in common law countries.

The fact that these two legal traditions are of European origin should give us pause. There are, of course, many other legal traditions in today's world, and new ones are forming. The dominance of the two traditions of which we have spoken is the direct result of European imperialism in earlier centuries, just as the dominance of Roman law in an earlier age was a product of Roman imperialism.

Historians are used to dealing with the coexistence of permanence and change in human affairs. Although we do not here purport to be writing legal history, our discussion of the civil law tradition necessarily treats it as something that endures, even as particular elements of the legal systems that share that tradition rise, fall, and evolve. The civil law tradition we describe would not be recognizable to lawyers in France or Spain in the eighteenth century, just as Wall Street lawyers are quite different from the serjeants-at-law in Elizabethan times. Change and permanence in the traditions are some of the issues we discuss in this book.

II

ROMAN CIVIL LAW, CANON LAW,
AND COMMERCIAL LAW

WE HAVE been discussing the civil law tradition as though it were homogeneous. Now we must face the unhappy fact that it is really not that simple. The civil law tradition is a composite of several distinct elements or subtraditions, with separate origins and developments in different periods of history. In this and the next few chapters these subtraditions are described under the following headings: Roman civil law, canon law, commercial law, the revolution, and legal science. A brief discussion of each of them provides a convenient way of summarizing the historical development of the civil law tradition and indicating something of the complexity of that tradition.

The oldest subtradition is directly traceable to the Roman law as compiled and codified under Justinian in the sixth century AD. It includes the law of persons, the family, inheritance, property, torts, unjust enrichment, and contracts and the remedies by which interests falling into these categories are judicially protected. Although the rules actually in force have changed, often drastically, since 533, the first three books of the Institutes of Justinian (Of Persons, Of Things, Of Obligations) and the major nineteenth-century civil codes all deal with substantially the same sets of problems and relationships, and the substantive area they cover is what a civil lawyer calls "civil law." The belief that this group of subjects is a related body of law that constitutes the fundamental content of the legal system is deeply rooted in Europe and the other parts of the world that have received the civil law tradition, and it is one of the principal distinguishing marks of what common lawyers call the civil law system. The expansion of governmental activity and the increasing importance of public law have not seriously altered this outlook. "Civil law" is still fundamental law to most civil lawyers. Hence there is a problem of terminology. Common lawyers use the term "civil law" to refer to the entire legal system in nations falling within the civil law tradition. But the legal terminology of lawyers within such a jurisdiction uses "civil law" to refer to that portion of the legal

6

system just described. The problem will be dealt with in this book by using the term "Roman civil law" to refer to this part of the law.

Justinian, a Roman emperor residing in Constantinople, had two principal motivations when he ordered the preparation, under the guidance of the jurist Tribonian, of what is now called the *Corpus Juris Civilis*. First, Justinian was a reactionary: he considered the contemporary Roman law decadent; he sought to rescue the Roman legal system from several centuries of deterioration and restore it to its former purity and grandeur. Second, he was a codifier: the mass of authoritative and quasi-authoritative material had become so great, and included so many refinements and different points of view, that it seemed desirable to Justinian to eliminate that which was wrong, obscure, or repetitive; to resolve conflicts and doubts; and to organize what was worth retaining into some systematic form. In particular, Justinian was concerned about the great number, length, and variety of commentaries and treatises written by legal scholars (called jurisconsults). He sought both to abolish the authority of all but the greatest of the jurisconsults of the classical period and to make it unnecessary for any more commentaries or treatises to be written.

On publication of the *Corpus Juris Civilis*, Justinian forbade any further reference to the works of jurisconsults. Those of their works that he approved were included in the *Corpus Juris Civilis*, and henceforward reference was to be made to it, rather than to the original authorities. He also forbade the preparation of any commentaries on his compilation itself. In other words, he sought to abolish all prior law except that included in the *Corpus Juris Civilis*, and he took the view that what was in his compilation would be adequate for the solution of legal problems without the aid of further interpretations or commentary by legal scholars. He was able to make his prohibition against citation of the original authorities more effective by having some of the manuscripts of their work, which had been collected by Tribonian, burned. The prohibition against citation of works not included in the *Corpus Juris Civilis* effectively destroyed an even greater amount of material, because it naturally diminished interest in preserving and copying the works of the jurisconsults who had produced them. (These two influences have, understandably, complicated the work of persons interested in studying the pre-Justinian Roman law). His command that there be no commentaries on the compilation was less effective, however, and was disregarded during his lifetime.

The *Corpus Juris Civilis* of Justinian is a complex work. It includes the *Digest*, which is a compilation of opinions of great jurisconsults of the classical era (100 BC to AD 250). This is by far the most important part and caught the attention of medieval jurists. The *Code* and *Novellae* are compilations of edicts and rescripts of emperors, including Justinian. These books cover the issues related to the power of the emperor, the organization of the empire, and a variety of other matters that lawyers today would classify as public law. They have been less important in the study of Roman law. The remaining part was the *Institutes*, a teaching book, which was essentially a new edition of Gaius's work (c. AD 170). As this book was relatively simple and well organized, it became the center of attention in seventeenth and eighteenth centuries and, thanks to commentaries of that time, was presented as a compendium of reason.

If we look at its immediate impact, Justinian's work was a failure: its stated purposes were not achieved, and it was forgotten for five centuries. In fact, it had a much greater importance: he succeeded in changing the Roman idea of law. For Roman jurisconsults the law was product of experience, a search for a just solution to a conflict or a possible conflict of interests. Justinian transformed the law in a written rule approved by the political power. But he succeeded many centuries after his death: the law became a written text. His work became the center of the study of law in Europe for several centuries. It became the core of the civil law tradition.

With the fall of the Roman Empire in the West in AD 476, Roman law lost its dynamism. Cruder, less sophisticated versions of the Roman civil law were applied by the invaders to the peoples of the Italian Peninsula and other parts of Europe. The invaders also brought with them their own Germanic legal customs, which, under their rule that the law of a person's nationality followed him wherever he went, were applied to themselves but not to those they had conquered. Even so, a fusion of some Germanic tribal laws with indigenous Roman legal institutions did take place in parts of Italy, southern France, and the Iberian Peninsula. Over the centuries this produced what Europeans still refer to as a "vulgarized" or "barbarized" Roman law, which is today of interest primarily to legal historians. Justinian's project was not only a revival of the Roman law but also the revival of the empire. He was the emperor of the Eastern part, or Byzantium. His ambitious attempt to regain the Italian Peninsula fell short, and what is today Western Europe stayed in the hands of Germanic invaders, except in Spain, where the Visigoths were succeeded by the Arabs.

As the Europeans regained control of the Mediterranean Sea, an extraordinary period of feverish intellectual and artistic rebirth called the Medieval Renaissance (or the Renaissance of the twelfth century) began, and an intellectual and scholarly interest in law reappeared. What civil lawyers commonly refer to as "the revival of Roman law" is generally conceded to have had its beginning in Bologna, Italy, late in the eleventh century. There was, however, an earlier revival of interest in the *Corpus Juris Civilis* in the ninth century, in the Eastern Roman Empire, resulting in the publication (in Greek) of a compilation called the *Basilica*. Although the *Basilica* had much less general influence than the subsequent Italian revival, it remained an important source of civil law in Greece until the adoption of the first Greek civil code after World War II.

The first modern European university appeared at Bologna, and law was a major object of study. But the law that was studied was not the barbarized Roman law that had been in force under the Germanic invaders. Nor was it the body of rules enacted or customarily followed by local towns, merchants' guilds, or petty sovereigns. The law studied was the *Corpus Juris Civilis* of Justinian.

There were several reasons for this attention to the *Corpus Juris Civilis* and neglect of other available bodies of law. First was the conception of knowledge characteristic of medieval Europe that "we are dwarfs on giants' shoulders." The ancient wisdom of the giants was contained in great books: the Bible, the works of the church fathers, Aristotle's works. The great law book was the *Corpus Juris Civilis*, and especially the *Digest*. Its content was Roman law, the law of the empire and the church (because the church lived under Roman law). As such it had the authority of both the pope and the temporal emperor behind it. This made it far superior in force and range of applicability to the legislation of a local prince, the regulations of a guild, or local custom.

Second, the jurists recognized the high intellectual quality of the *Corpus Juris Civilis*. They saw that this work, which they called "written reason," was superior to the barbarized compilations that had come into use under the Germanic invaders. The *Corpus Juris Civilis* carried not only the authority of the pope and the emperor but also the authority of an obviously superior civilization and intelligence.

9

Within a short time, Bologna and the other universities of northern Italy became the legal center of the Western world. Men came from all over Europe to study the law as taught in the Italian universities. The law studied was the *Corpus Juris Civilis,* and the common language of study was Latin. There was a succession of schools of thought about the proper way to study and explain the *Corpus Juris Civilis.* Of special prominence, for both their views of the law and their styles of scholarship, were the groups of scholars known as the glossators and the commentators. They produced an immense literature, which itself became the object of study and discussion and came to carry great authority.

Those who had studied in Bologna returned to their nations and established universities where they also taught and studied the law of the *Corpus Juris Civilis* according to the style of the glossators and commentators. In this way, the Roman civil law and the works of the glossators and commentators became the basis of a common law of Europe, which is actually called the *jus commune* by legal historians. There was a common body of law and of writing about law, a common legal language, and a common method of teaching and scholarship. It was called the *mos italicus.* In England, the *Corpus Juris Civilis* was taught at Oxford and Cambridge, and the lawyers educated there were called civil lawyers. They had the exclusive privilege of litigation in the Court of Chancery (or court of equity), which had the mission of correcting the rigidity and limitation of the English common law. In this way, the common law received the influence of Roman law.

Eventually, in France in the sixteenth century, legal scholars who came to be called humanists criticized the *Digest* as a disorganized and obscurely casuist book. They emphasized humanism and rationalism and turned their attention to Justinian's *Institutes,* a shorter, systematic work originally intended as a textbook on law. Jean Domat crowned their effort in a book called *The Civil Law in Its Natural Order,* which was a rationalization of Roman law.

The rise of nation-states and the growing power of kings provided a significant opportunity for university-educated jurists. They were the intellectuals who staffed the royal bureaucracies that were the kings' instruments of power. To those officials, the true law resided in the ancient texts they had studied in the universities. They did not consider royal legislation constitutive of law but treated it rather as a kind of interpretation. Thus, ironically, Roman law and the *jus commune* grew and thrived during the rise of the nation-state.

In some parts of Europe (e.g., Germany), the Roman civil law and the writings of the Bolognese scholars were formally "received" as binding law. (Civil lawyers use the term "reception" to sum up the process by which the nation-states of the civil law world came to include the *jus commune* in their national legal systems.) In other parts of Europe, the reception was less formal; the *Corpus Juris Civilis* and the works of the glossators and commentators were recognized as authoritative because of their appeal as an intellectually superior system. But by one means or another, the Roman civil law was received throughout a large part of Western Europe, in the nations that are now the home of the civil law tradition.

In the nineteenth century, the principal states of Western Europe adopted civil codes (as well as other codes), of which the French Code of 1804 (also called Code Napoléon) is the archetype. The subject matter of these civil codes was almost identical to the subject matter of the first three books of the Institutes of Justinian and the Roman civil law component of the *jus commune* of medieval Europe. The principal concepts were Roman law or rationalized Roman law, and the organization and conceptual structure were similar. A European or Latin American civil code of today clearly demonstrates the influence of Roman law and its medieval and modern revival. Roman civil law epitomizes the oldest, most continuously and thoroughly studied, and (in the opinion of civil lawyers) most basic part of the civil law tradition.

Roman law is often said to be the greatest contribution that Rome has made to Western civilization, and Roman ways of thinking have certainly percolated into every Western legal system. In this sense, all Western lawyers are Roman lawyers. In civil law nations, however, the influence of Roman civil law is much more pervasive, direct, and concrete than it is in the common law world.

The second oldest component of the civil law tradition is the canon law of the Roman Catholic Church. The canon law had its beginnings early in the Christian era and has a fascinating history, including forged documents treated for centuries as though they were genuine. Various collections and arrangements of canon law materials were assembled, and by the time of the Bolognese revival, a substantial body of written canon law was available for study. Gratian's *Decretum*, itself a compilation, was for the canon law what the *Digest* was for Roman law.

This body of law and procedure was developed by the church for its own governance and to regulate the rights and obligations of its communicants. Just as the Roman civil law was the universal law of the temporal empire, directly associated with the authority of the emperor, so the canon law was the universal law of the spiritual domain, directly associated with the authority of the Catholic Church. The Bible was the most cited book in Gratian's *Decretum* and the inspiration for many of its rules. In canon law development, the religious inspiration weakened but a certain moralism remained.

In practice, however, the distinctions between different types of law were less clear. Royal courts that were supposed to apply royal laws were staffed by university-educated jurists who were trained in and naturally favored Roman law. Seigniorial courts that applied customary law also felt the influence of educated jurists. Ecclesiastical courts were staffed with canon law judges who were university educated in both canon and Roman law. There was a tendency of overlapping jurisdiction. Ecclesiastical courts frequently exercised jurisdiction in family law and succession matters, as well as in certain types of crimes.

The study of canon law was joined with the study of the Roman civil law in the universities of the civil law world. Students studied "both laws." The degree conferred on a student who had completed the full course of study was Utriusque Juris Doctor, or doctor of both laws, referring to the civil law and the canon law. (The JUD degree is still granted in some universities in the civil law world.) Because the two were studied together in the universities, there was a tendency for them to influence each other; and the canon law, as well as the Roman civil law, helped in the formation of the *jus commune* that was subsequently received by the European states.

Canon law influenced the *jus commune* mainly in the areas of family law and succession (both parts of the Roman civil law), criminal law, and the law of procedure. By the time the ecclesiastical courts of Europe were deprived of their civil jurisdiction, many substantive and procedural principles and institutions they had developed had been adopted by the royal courts themselves.

This Roman civil law–canon law *jus commune* was the generally applicable law of Europe. There was also, of course, a great amount of local law, some of it customary and some in the form of legislation by princes, lords, towns, or communes. In general, such law was regarded as exceptional in nature and of only local interest. The attention of the legal scholar was focused on the *jus commune*

12

rather than on local variations. Still, local law had some effect on the development of the *jus commune*. Many of the most important law teachers and scholars were also practicing lawyers in constant contact with the law in action. What they saw of customary and local law, particularly in fields such as criminal law, where Roman law was undeveloped or considered inapplicable, helped form their ideas about the *jus commune*. At the same time their scholarly bent and their conviction of the superiority of Roman civil law strongly affected the development of local law. The two tended to converge along lines favored by the scholars.

The reception of the *jus commune* in European nations eventually aroused a nationalistic concern for the identification and preservation—and in some cases the glorification—of indigenous legal institutions. The *coutumes* of the various French regions generally classified as the *pays de droit coutumier* (regions of customary law)—in contrast to those regions generally classified as *pays de droit écrit* (regions of written law), where Roman law was the dominant influence—became a source of national pride and scholarly interest as France became self-consciously a nation-state. After the French Revolution, an effort was made during codification to include institutions from the *coutumes* in the new centralized legal order. In Germany a dispute arose during the preparatory work of codification between the so-called Germanists and Romanists, and the draft of a civil code originally proposed for unified Germany was rejected because of the opposition of the Germanists. Their complaint was that the draft was purely Roman in form and substance, to the neglect of native legal institutions, and they were able to force a revision for the purpose of giving the code a more German, less purely Roman, flavor.

In these and other ways, the development of a national legal system in each of the major European nations took on certain characteristics directly traceable to the desire to identify, perpetuate, and glorify indigenous legal institutions. This tendency is indeed one of the main reasons for the substantial differences that exist between contemporary civil law systems. But what binds such nations together is that these indigenous legal institutions have been combined with the form and substance of Roman civil law, under the influence of the *jus commune*. The Roman influence is very great; the native legal contribution, while substantial, is generally of subsidiary importance. It does not go to such matters as basic legal attitudes and notions, or to the organization and style of the legal order. These are drawn from the older, more fully developed and sophisticated Roman civil law tradition. The language and principles of law are basically Roman.

The third subtradition, after Roman civil law and canon law, is commercial law. Although it is obvious that some form of commercial law is as old as commerce, the commercial law of Western Europe (and also, as it happens, of the common law world) had its principal development in Italy at the time of the Crusades, when European commerce regained dominance in the Mediterranean area. Italian merchants formed guilds and established rules for the conduct of commercial affairs. Medieval Italian towns became commercial centers, and the rules developed within these towns—particularly Amalfi, Genoa, Pisa, and Venice—were influential in the development of commercial law. Unlike Roman civil law and canon law, which were bookish and dominated by scholars, commercial law was the pragmatic creation of practical men engaged in commerce. Interpretation and application of the commercial law went on in commercial courts, in which the judges were merchants. The needs of commerce and the interests of merchants, not the compilation of Justinian or those of the canonists, were the main sources of the law. Nevertheless, the merchant judges consulted educated jurists as a way of avoiding conflict with royal courts. In this way, Roman law language and institutions influenced commercial law.

The commercial law that developed out of the activities of the guilds and of the maritime cities soon became international in character. It became a common commercial law that penetrated throughout the commercial world, even into areas, such as England, where the Roman civil law had met with resistance. This common commercial law of Europe was later received by the nation-states and eventually was incorporated into the commercial codes adopted throughout the civil law world in the eighteenth and nineteenth centuries.

These three subtraditions within the civil law tradition—Roman civil law, canon law, and commercial law—are the principal historical sources of the concepts, institutions, and procedures of most of the private law and procedural law, and much of the criminal law of modern civil law systems. In modern form, as affected by revolutionary law and legal science (described in the next few chapters), they are embodied in the five basic codes typically found in a civil law jurisdiction: the civil code, the commercial code, the code of civil procedure, the penal code, and the code of criminal procedure.

III

THE REVOLUTION

THREE OF the five principal subtraditions of the civil law tradition—Roman civil law, canon law, and commercial law—are, as we have seen, the historical sources of much of the law embodied in the five basic codes in force in most civil law jurisdictions. The reader will observe that much of public law, particularly constitutional law and administrative law, is conspicuously absent from this listing. The reason is that the public law in contemporary civil law nations is in large part a product of a revolution that took place in the West in the century beginning with the year 1776. This movement, which affected most Western nations, included such dramatic events as the American and French revolutions, the Italian Risorgimento, the independence movements that liberated the nations of Latin America, the unification of Germany under Otto von Bismarck, and the liberation of Greece after centuries of Turkish domination.

But these events were themselves related to a more fundamental intellectual and social revolution. Certain long-established patterns of thought about government and the individual were finally overcome, and newer ways of thinking about humanity, society, the economy, and the state took their place. Even in parts of the West that escaped violent revolutions (e.g., England), these newer ideas came to prevail. It is in this intellectual revolution that we find the main sources of public law in the civil law tradition. Although a careful historical investigation could undoubtedly trace the origin of several contemporary governmental institutions to legal materials that preceded this revolution, the fact is that the guiding spirit of European public law and many of the concepts and institutions in which it is expressed are of modern origin and do not have deep roots in the Roman or medieval periods of European history.

The effect of the revolution was not, however, limited to public law. It also had a profound influence on the form, the method of application, and, to a lesser extent, the content of the basic codes derived from Roman and *jus commune* sources. The intellectual

15

revolution produced a new way of thinking about law that had important consequences for the organization and administration of the legal system and for rules of substantive and procedural law.

One of the principal driving intellectual forces of the revolution was what has since come to be called secular natural law ("secular" because it was not derived from religious doctrine, belief, or authority). Revolutionary thought was severely antireligious and anticlerical. It was based on certain ideas about man's nature that find expression in the American Declaration of Independence and in the French Declaration of the Rights of Man and of the Citizen. All men, so the reasoning goes, are created equal. They have certain natural rights to property, to liberty, to life. The proper function of government is to recognize and secure those rights and to ensure equality among men. Government should be carried on by elected representatives. And so on.

On the contrary, the leading principle of the ancien régime was inequality. In a rigid stratified society, each individual has a more or less permanent position, a *status*. There was an aristocracy related to land ownership, but there were aristocracies of other kinds based on other considerations, such at the aristocracy of the robe. Before the French Revolution, judicial offices were regarded as property that one could buy, sell, and leave to an heir upon one's death. Montesquieu himself inherited such an office, held it for a decade, and sold it. The judges were an aristocratic group who supported the landed aristocracy against the peasants and the urban working and middle classes, and against the centralization of governmental power in Paris. Church people also enjoyed many privileges. The principle of inequality was clearly inconsistent with the new ideas. When the French Revolution came, the landed aristocracy fell, and with it the aristocracy of the robe. Clerics also lost most privileges.

A second tenet of the intellectual revolution was the separation of governmental powers. A number of writers, notably Montesquieu in his *Spirit of the Laws*, had persuasively argued the fundamental importance to rational government of establishing and maintaining a separation of governmental powers, and in particular of clearly distinguishing and separating the legislative and the executive, on the one hand, from the judiciary, on the other. The purpose was to prevent intrusion of the judiciary into areas—lawmaking and the execution of the laws—reserved to the other two powers. This attitude toward the judicial power did not exist in the United States either before or

16

after the American Revolution. The system of checks and balances that has emerged in the United States places no special emphasis on isolating the judiciary, and it proceeds from a philosophy different from that which produced the sharp separation of powers customarily encountered in the civil law world. It is important to emphasize this point and to understand why this was the case.

In France the judicial aristocracy were targets of the Revolution not only because of their tendency to identify with the landed aristocracy but also because of their failure to distinguish very clearly between applying law and making law. As a result of these failings, efforts by the Crown to unify the kingdom and to enforce relatively enlightened and progressive legislative reforms had frequently been frustrated. The courts refused to apply the new laws, interpreted them contrary to their intent, or hindered the attempts of officials to administer them. Montesquieu and others developed the theory that the only sure way of preventing abuses of this kind was first to separate the legislative and executive from the judicial power, and then to regulate the judiciary carefully to ensure that it restricted itself to applying the law made by the legislature and did not interfere with public officials performing their administrative functions.

In the United States and England, however, there was a different kind of judicial tradition, one in which judges had often been a progressive force on the side of the individual against the abuse of power by the ruler and had played an important part in the centralization of governmental power and the destruction of feudalism. The fear of judicial lawmaking and of judicial interference in administration did not exist. On the contrary, the power of the judges to shape the development of the common law was a familiar and welcome institution. It was accepted that the courts had the powers of mandamus (to compel officials to perform their legal duty) and quo warranto (to question the legality of an act performed by a public official). The judiciary was not a target of the American Revolution in the way that it was in France.

The age was also the Age of Reason. Rationalism was a dominant intellectual force. It was assumed that reason controlled human activities and that all obstacles would fall before the proper exercise of careful thought. The subconscious had not yet been discovered, and the power of irrational forces in history was not yet recognized. It was optimistically assumed that existing laws and institutions could be repealed and new ones, rationally derived from unimpeachable first principles, put in their place.

17

The emphasis on the rights of man in the revolutionary period produced statements about individual liberty of the sort found in the American Declaration of Independence and in the French Declaration of the Rights of Man and of the Citizen. There was, however, a very important difference. Feudalism (in the general, nontechnical sense of the term as it was used by many European and Latin American revolutionaries) had survived in Europe and Latin America in a form that kept alive many of the social injustices inherent in its origins, whereas in the American colonies, legal institutions of undeniably feudal origin had already been deprived of much of their ability to produce the kind of social and economic evils that characterized feudal societies. As a consequence, the intellectual revolution in the civil law world was more intensely antifeudal in orientation than it was in the United States. The emphasis on the right of an individual to own property and on the obligation of the law to protect that ownership was in part a reaction against dependent tenure under feudalism. The emphasis on an individual's right to conduct his own affairs and to move laterally and vertically in society was a reaction against the tendency under feudalism to fix a person in a place and status. The revolution became, to use Sir Henry Maine's famous phrase, an instrument for the transition "from status to contract." The result was an exaggerated emphasis on private property and liberty of contract, similar in effect to the exaggerated individualism of nineteenth-century England and America. But the reaction in the civil law world carried a special antifeudal flavor.

The revolution was also a great step along the path toward glorification of the secular state. Henceforward the temporal allegiance of the individual would be owed primarily to the state. Feudal obligations and relationships were abolished. Religious obligations lost most of their remaining legal importance. The ecclesiastical courts lost what little remained of their temporal jurisdiction. Family relationships were now defined and regulated by law (i.e., by the state). Local governmental autonomies were abolished; guilds and corporations were deprived of regulatory power. Separate legal traditions were merged into a single body of national law. The legal universe, formerly very complicated, was suddenly simplified: henceforward it would in theory be inhabited only by the individual and the monolithic state.

Nationalism was another aspect of the glorification of the state. The objective was a national legal system that would express national ideals and the unity of the nation's culture. Such a national law should be expressed in a national language and should incorporate national legal institutions and concepts. The authority (but not the content) of the *jus commune* was rejected; a common law of the civil law world was now history. In the future all law would be national law, and variation from the *jus commune* was not merely accepted; it was valued as evidence of national genius and identity.

Thus the revolution was composed of such intellectual forces as natural rights, the separation of powers, rationalism, antifeudalism, bourgeois liberalism, statism, and nationalism. These are all respectable enough as ideas or points of view, so long as they are kept in proportion. But during and following the revolution a general atmosphere of exaggeration prevailed (as is typical of revolutionary movements). The hated past was painted in excessively dark colors. The objectives of the revolution were idealized and the possibility of their accomplishment assumed. The problems in the way of reform were ignored or oversimplified. Ideological passion displaced reason; revolutionary ideas became dogmas; the revolution became utopian.

In France in particular, just as in the Soviet Union after the October Revolution, the utopian flavor was very strong. Tocqueville said that the revolution "developed into a species of religion." This development profoundly affected the revolutionary reforms in France, and since the revolutionary law of France has been extremely influential outside of France, the legal systems in many parts of the civil law world show the effects both of the fervent utopianism that characterized the French Revolution and of reactions against it. The emphasis on separation of powers led to a separate system of administrative courts, inhibited the adoption of judicial review of legislation, and limited the judge to a relatively minor role in the legal process. The theory of natural rights led to an exaggerated emphasis on individual rights of property and contract and to an oversharp distinction between public and private law. Glorification of the state, nationalism, and rationalism combined to produce a peculiar civil law theory of what law is and to determine the form and style of the basic codes.

IV

THE SOURCES OF LAW

THE POLYCENTRIC, highly decentralized, complex, and inefficient structure of the medieval political world fell before the need for a more efficient, centralized governmental system—the modern nation-state. Both to bring about this kind of transformation and to consolidate the accomplishments of the revolution, an ideology was needed, and nationalism—the ideology of the state—met this need. And if nationalism was the prevailing ideology, sovereignty was the basic premise of its legal expression.

The concept of sovereignty had existed for several centuries. Its development as a legal concept can be traced to the work of certain thinkers, notably the Frenchman Jean Bodin, the Dutchman Hugh Grotius, and the Englishman Thomas Hobbes. Bodin and Hobbes focused on internal sovereignty: the supremacy of the state, free of any external restraint, to order its relations with its citizens. Grotius, who is often called the "father of international law," looked more to the relation among states. His work in international law both supported the claims and attempted to control the conduct of the colonial and empire-building powers.

Another dimension of the movement toward state positivism was provided by the secular character of the revolutions in Europe. Although there were variations in form and degree from nation to nation, the idea that law was of divine origin—whether expressed directly, as in divine (i.e., scriptural) law, or expressed indirectly through the nature of human beings as created by God, as in Roman Catholic natural law—had lost most of its remaining vitality. Formal respect might still be paid to the deity in the lawmaking process (as, for example, in the American Declaration of Independence), but the operating theory had become that the ultimate lawmaking power lay in the state. Roman Catholic natural law had lost its power to control the prince. Secular natural law, while providing many of the ideas that were the intellectual fuel of the revolution, was ineffectual as a control on the activity of the state. It was backed by no organization and had no sanctioning power. The perennial controversy between natural lawyers and legal positivists (familiar to all students of legal philosophy) thus was decisively resolved, for operational purposes at least, in favor of the positivists. Consequently, although this debate still goes on, it has had a distinctly academic flavor since the emergence of the modern state. All Western states had become positivistic, at least until the age of globalization.

The emergence of the modern nation-state destroyed the legal unity provided by common acceptance of the Roman-canonic *jus commune* in feudal and early modern Europe. The *jus commune*, associated for many with the concept of the Holy Roman Empire, was a law that transcended the diversities of local communities and nations. With the decay of feudalism, the advent of the Reformation, and the consequent weakening of the authority of the pope and the Holy Roman Empire, the centralized monarchy began to emerge as the principal claimant to citizens' loyalty. The centralized state stood in opposition both to the medieval autonomy of classes and lands commonly associated with feudalism and to every kind of power outside the state. The state tended to become the unique source of law, claiming sovereignty for itself both internally and internationally. Thus, national legal systems began to replace the *jus commune*, which became a subordinate or supplementary law. Late Roman law itself was quoted as providing, in the maxim *quod principi placuit legis habet vigorem* (the prince's pleasure is law), justification for the legal autonomy of the state that led eventually to its displacement in favor of national legal systems. The authority of the prince replaced that of the *jus commune*. The content of national law might continue to be drawn largely from the *jus commune*, but its authority came from the state.

So began the age of absolute sovereignty. The authority of state law depended on the will of the prince. Law from other sources, such as the *jus commune* or established custom, was applied because the prince so willed it. Princes also legislated, and the process of building a national law, usually in the national language, proceeded on the basis of assumptions that presaged European legal positivism. The legislative act was subject to no authority, temporal or spiritual, superior to the state, nor was it subject to any limitation from within the state, such as local or customary law. From a time when lawmaking was distributed along a spectrum running from the local lord or town council through the emperor and the universal church, the West had moved to lawmaking at only one point: the centralized nation-state. Sovereignty had two faces, an outer face that excluded any law of external origin and an inner face that excluded any law of local or customary origin.

It is important to understand that state positivism was much more sharply and consciously emphasized on the Continent than it was in England during this period of revolutionary change. One reason, of course, was the milder, more gradual, and more evolutionary nature of the revolution in England. There, many of the forms of feudalism were retained, although their substance was transformed. The trappings of an established church survived, but that church's influence on the form and content of lawmaking diminished to its vanishing point. Most important of all, the indigenous common law of England, which had developed along lines quite different from those taken by the *jus commune* on the Continent, was not rejected in the interest of statism, nationalism, positivism, and sovereignty. On the contrary, the common law of England was a positive force in the emergence of England as a nation-state, and it was vigorously embraced as evidence of national identity and national genius. The Roman and continental connections were greatly reduced. On the Continent, revolution seemed to require a rejection of the old legal order; in England, it seemed to require acceptance and even glorification of it. The implications of this difference for the attitudes toward codification in the civil law and common law worlds are obvious. On the Continent, where it was thought necessary to reject the *jus commune*, it was natural that new legal systems were codified; in England, where it was thought necessary to retain the common law, there seemed no need for codification.

On the Continent the rejection of the old order proceeded along the lines indicated by a vision of the world as properly organized into secular, positivistic nation-states. Consequently, the natural law of the Roman Catholic Church, like other externally derived theories of law and justice, and the canon law, like other external bodies of rules and institutions, could not have effect as law within the state. The Western school of international law, which is based on a kind of absolute sovereignty of the state that permits it to be bound only when it agrees to be, treated even accepted principles of international law as operative within the state only if the state itself decided that they should be. The law produced by international organizations and the obligations of members of such organizations again affected the state only if it had agreed to be subject to them. The laws of one state could be enforced within another state only if the latter chose to permit their enforcement. A judgment rendered by a court of one state would or would not be enforced by the courts of another state at the latter's option. The outward face of state positivism was thus uniform and unbroken: nothing outside the state could make law effective on or within the state without the state's consent.

The inner face of the school of state positivism was equally unbroken. Only the state had lawmaking power, and hence no individual or group within the state could produce law. The ability of individuals to bind themselves by contracts and of the members of organizations to adopt effective rules governing their internal relations did not give them lawmaking power. These were considered private arrangements, which had legal effect only to the extent that the state chose to recognize and enforce them. Books and articles written by scholars (although much more influential than legal scholarship in common law countries, as will be explained in Chapter IX) also were not law, for the same reasons.

Thus, state positivism, as expressed in the dogma of the absolute external and internal sovereignty of the state, led to a state monopoly on lawmaking. Revolutionary emphasis on the strict separation of powers demanded that only specifically designated organs of the state be entitled to make law. According to that doctrine, the legislative and judicial powers of the government were different in kind; to prevent abuse, they had to be very sharply separated from each other. The legislative power is by definition the lawmaking power, and hence only the legislature could make law. As the only representative, directly elected branch of the government, the legislature alone could respond to the popular will. Some of the consequences of this dogma for the civil law judge are discussed in the next chapter. For now, it need be said only that the familiar common law doctrine of stare decisis—that is, the power and obligation of courts to base decisions on prior decisions—is obviously inconsistent with the separation of powers as formulated in civil law countries and is therefore rejected by the civil law tradition. Judicial decisions are not law.

What, then, was law? The basic answer, which is the essence of legislative positivism, is that only statutes enacted by the legislative power could be law. In theory, the legislature might enact anything. In practice, however, there were limits, the most important of which were imposed by the concepts, categories, and principles of the Roman law that was still taught in the universities and revered as "written reason."

Before the revolution the legislature could no more supersede Roman law than it could supersede geometry or mathematics. But the authority of Roman law gradually declined as legislation gained strength, and in the nineteenth century law became synonymous with legislation. The legislature could delegate some of that power to the executive, and it could give administrative agencies the power to issue regulations having the force of law, but such "delegated legislation" was in theory effective only within the limits provided in the delegating legislation. The legislative power was supreme.

In addition to statutes (including legislation promulgated by the executive under delegated powers) and administrative regulations, nations with the civil law tradition still commonly recognize a third source of law, called custom. Where a person acts in accordance with custom under the assumption that it represents the law, that action will be accepted as legal in many civil law jurisdictions, so long as there is no applicable statute or regulation to the contrary. The amount of writing on custom as law in civil law jurisdictions is immense, far out of proportion to its actual importance as law. The main reason for so much writing (in addition to the importance of custom as a source of law in the earlier history of the civil law tradition) is the need to justify treating as law something that is not created by the legislative power of the state. To give custom the force of law would appear to violate the dogma of state positivism (only the state can make law) and the dogma of sharp separation of powers (within the state only the legislature can make law). Some very sophisticated theories have been developed to explain away this apparent inconsistency. Meanwhile, the importance of custom as a source of law is slight and decreasing.

The result of all this is that the accepted theory of sources of law in the civil law tradition recognizes only statutes, regulations, and custom as sources of law. This listing is exclusive. It is also arranged in descending order of authority. A statute prevails over a contrary regulation. Both a statute and a regulation prevail over an inconsistent custom. This may all seem very technical and of dubious importance, but in fact it is basic to our understanding of the civil law tradition, because the function of judges in that tradition is to interpret and to apply "the law" as it is technically defined in their jurisdiction. Both state positivism and the dogma of separation of powers require that judges resort only to "the law" in the deciding of cases. It is assumed that whatever the problem that may come before them, judges will be able to find some form of law to apply—whether a statute, a regulation, or an applicable custom. They cannot turn to books and articles by legal scholars or to prior judicial decisions for the law.

This dogmatic conception of what law, like many other implications of the dogmas of the revolutionary period, has been eroded by time and events. Perhaps the most spectacular innovation has been the strong movement toward constitutionalism, with its emphasis on the functional rigidity—and hence superiority as a source of law—of written constitutions. Such constitutions, by eliminating the power of the legislature to amend by ordinary legislative action, impair the legislature's monopoly on lawmaking. They insert a new element into the hierarchy of sources of law, which now must read "constitution, legislation, regulations, and custom." In addition, if a court can decide that a statute is void because it is in conflict with the constitution, the dogma of sharp separation of legislative power from judicial power is impaired. The power of judicial review of the constitutionality of legislative action has long existed in Mexico and most other Latin American nations (although it was not always aggressively exercised). And since World War II, judicial review, in one form or another, has appeared in practically every country. As the constitution does not speak by itself, this addition has increased judges' power, especially in constitutional courts or supreme courts.

Another complicating factor is the inclusion of the initiative and the referendum in the constitutions of some civil law countries; this necessarily involves the transfer of some lawmaking power from the legislature to the people and further weakens the position of the legislature as the sole source of law. The growth of international and supranational organizations, including courts, as well as the trend in Europe and Latin America toward the transfer of some legislative power to such organizations, further weakens the traditional theory. In Chapter VI, on judges, we describe the various ways in which this theory of sources of law has been subverted by the conduct of civil law judges.

These and other modern tendencies have been noted by scholars, who have often recognized their implications for the orthodox theory of sources of law, but the tendencies do not seriously impair the more generally prevailing view of what law is. To the average judge, lawyer, or law student in France or Argentina, for example, the traditional theory of sources of law represents the basic truth. It is a part of his or her ideology.

In the common law world, however, a world less compelled by the peculiar history and the rationalist dogmas of the French Revolution, quite different attitudes prevail. The common law of England, an unsystematic accretion of statutes, judicial decisions, and customary practices, is thought of as the major source of law. It has deep historical dimensions and is not the product of a conscious revolutionary attempt to make or to restate the applicable law at a moment in history. There is no systematic, hierarchical theory of sources of law: legislation, of course, is law, but so are other things, including judicial decisions. In formal terms the relative authority of statutes, regulations, and judicial decisions might run in roughly that order, but in practice such formulations tend to lose their neatness and importance. Common lawyers tend to be much less rigorous about such matters than civil lawyers. The attitudes that led France to adopt the metric system, decimal currency, legal codes, and a rigid theory of sources of law, all in the space of a few years, are still basically alien to the common law tradition.

V

CODES AND CODIFICATION

O NE OFTEN hears it said, sometimes by people who should know better, that civil law systems are codified statutory systems, whereas the common law is uncodified and is based in large part on judicial decisions. The purpose of this chapter is to indicate the extent to which this observation oversimplifies and misrepresents, and at the same time the extent to which it expresses, an important set of basic differences between the two legal traditions.

The distinction between legislative and judicial production of law can be misleading. There is probably at least as much legislation in force in a typical American state as there is in a typical European or Latin American nation. As in a civil law nation, legislation validly enacted in the United States is the law, which the judges are expected to interpret and apply in the spirit in which it was enacted. The authority of legislation is superior to that of judicial decisions; statutes supersede contrary judicial decisions (constitutional questions aside), but not vice versa. The amount of legislation and the degree of authority of legislation are not useful criteria for distinguishing civil law systems from common law systems.

Nor is the existence of something called a code a distinguishing criterion. For example, California has more codes than many civil law nations, but California is not a civil law jurisdiction. Codes do exist in most civil law systems, but bodies of systematic legislation covering broad areas of the law and indistinguishable in appearance from European or Latin American codes also exist in a number of common law nations. Conversely, codes appeared late—mostly in the nineteenth century—in the civil law tradition, and indeed a civil law system need not have codes at all. Hungary and Greece were civil law countries even before they enacted their civil codes: Hungarian civil law was uncodified until Hungary became a socialist state, and Greece enacted its first civil code after World War II. South Africa, whose legal system is based on Roman-Dutch law, is still uncodified, and citations of Justinian's *Digest* in South African judicial opinions are still encountered. The code form is thus not a distinctive identifying mark of a civil law system.

If, however, one thinks of codification not as a form but as the expression of an ideology, and if one tries to understand that ideology and why it achieves expression in code form, then one can see how it makes sense to talk about codes in comparative law. It is true that California has a number of what are called codes, as do some other states in the United States, and that the Uniform Commercial Code has been adopted in most American jurisdictions. However, although these look like the codes in civil law countries, the underlying ideology—the conception of what a code is and of the functions it should perform in the legal process—is not the same. There is an entirely different ideology of codification at work in the civil law world.

Recall that Justinian, when he promulgated the *Corpus Juris Civilis*, sought to abolish all prior law. Certain elements of the prior legal order were, however, included in the *Corpus Juris Civilis* itself, and were consequently preserved when he promulgated it. Similarly, the French, when they codified their law, repealed all prior law in the areas covered by the codes. Any principles of prior law that were incorporated in the codes received their validity not from their previous existence but from their incorporation and reenactment in codified form. Justinian and the French codifiers sought to destroy prior law for different but analogous reasons: Justinian sought to reestablish the purer law of an earlier time, the French to establish a new legal order. In both cases, the aims were essentially utopian. Let us look more closely at the utopia of the French codification.

The ideology of the French codification, though more temperate than that of the immediate postrevolutionary period, accurately reflects the ideology of the French Revolution. For example, one reason for the attempt to repeal all prior law, and thus limit the effect of law to new legislation, was statism—the glorification of the nation-state. A law that had its origins in an earlier time, before the creation of the state, violated this statist ideal. So did a law that had its origin outside the state—in the European *jus commune*. The nationalism of the time was also an important factor. Much of the prerevolutionary law in France was European rather than French in origin (the *jus commune*) and was consequently offensive to the rising spirit of French nationalism. At the same time, much that was French (the *coutumes* of the northern regions in particular) appeared as the logical object of preservation and glorification. The drive toward a centralized state made it important to bring unity out of the diversity of legal systems and materials in the French regions. The secular natural law ideal of one law applicable to all French citizens pointed the same way.

The rampant rationalism of the time also had an important effect on French codification. Only an exaggerated rationalism can explain the belief that history could be abolished by a repealing statute. Such an attitude is implicit also in the hypothesis that an entirely new legal system, incorporating only certain desirable aspects of the generally undesirable prior legal system, could be created and substituted for the old system. The assumption was that by reasoning from basic premises established by the thinkers of the secular natural law school, one could derive a legal system that would meet the needs of the new society and the new government. The legal scholars of the time were, of course, trained in an earlier period, and they found their working legal conceptions, institutions, and processes in the old law. Those who participated in drafting the French codes consequently incorporated a good deal of the prior law and legal learning into them. In this way some continuity with the prior legal culture was retained. This tempered the legal consequences of the French Revolution, but it did not entirely avoid them. For several decades after the enactment of the Code Napoléon (the French Civil Code of 1804), the fiction was stoutly maintained by a large group of French jurists that history was irrelevant to interpretation and application of the code. This point is illustrated by the frequently quoted statement of a French law professor of the period (Demolombe): "I know nothing of the civil law, I teach only the Code Napoléon."

As in many utopias, one of the objectives of the French Revolution was to make lawyers unnecessary. There was a desire for a legal system that was simple, nontechnical, and straightforward—one in which the professionalism and the tendency toward technicality and complication commonly blamed on lawyers could be avoided. One way to do this was to state the law clearly and in a straightforward fashion, so that ordinary citizens could read the law and understand what their rights and obligations were, without having to consult lawyers and go to court. Thus, the French Civil Code of 1804 was envisioned as a kind of popular book that could be put on the shelf next to the family Bible or, perhaps, in place of it. It would be a handbook for the citizen, clearly organized and stated in straightforward language that would enable citizens to determine their legal rights and obligations by themselves.

Fear of a *gouvernement des juges* hovered over French postrevolutionary reforms and colored the codification process. The emphasis on complete separation of powers, with all lawmaking power lodged in a representative legislature, was a way of ensuring that the judiciary would be denied lawmaking power. Experience with the prerevolutionary courts had made the French wary of judicial lawmaking disguised as interpretation of laws. Therefore, some writers argued that judges should be denied even the power to interpret legislation. (The history of this attitude and its subsequent relaxation are described in Chapter VII.) At the same time, however, judges had to decide every case that came before them. The premises of secular natural law required that justice be available to all. There could be no area for judicial selection or discretion in the exercise of jurisdiction.

But if the legislature alone could make laws and the judiciary could only apply them (or, at a later time, interpret and apply them), such legislation had to be complete, coherent, and clear. If judges were required to decide a case for which there was no legislative provision, they would in effect make law and thus violate the principle of separation of powers. Hence it was necessary that the legislature draft a code without gaps. Similarly, if there were conflicting provisions in the code, judges would make law by choosing one rather than another as more applicable to the situation. Hence there could be no conflicting provisions. Finally, if judges were allowed to decide which meaning to give to an ambiguous provision or an obscure statement, they would again be making law. Hence the code had to be clear.

If insistence on a total separation of legislative power from judicial power dictated that the codes be complete, coherent, and clear, the prevailing spirit of optimistic rationalism persuaded those in its spell that it was possible to draft systematic legislation that would have those characteristics to such a degree that the function of the judge would be limited to selecting the applicable provision of the code and giving it its obvious significance in the context of the case. Actually, the Code Napoléon is not the most extreme example of this type of codification. That dubious honor falls to the Prussian Landrecht of 1794, enacted under Frederick the Great and containing some seventeen thousand detailed provisions setting out precise rules to govern specific "fact situations." The French civil code was drafted by experienced and intelligent jurists who were familiar with the rather spectacular failure of the Prussian attempt to spell it all out. Indeed, if we read the comments of Jean-Étienne-Marie Portalis, one of the most influential of the drafters of the code, we find a constant realistic concern to avoid the extremes of rationalist ideology.

Portalis shows us that the code builds on much prerevolutionary law and legal scholarship; and he remarks that the provisions of the code are best thought of as principles or maxims, *féconds en conséquences*, to be developed and applied by judges and other jurists.

This kind of professional realism was, however, easily and quickly submerged by the rhetoric of the revolution and by the excesses of the prevailing rationalism. The code became a victim of the revolutionary ideology and was uniformly treated as though it were a conscious expression of that ideology, both in France and in the many nations in other parts of the world that were heavily influenced by the French Revolution.

In contrast to the essentially revolutionary, rationalistic, and nontechnical character of the Code Napoléon, the German Civil Code of 1896 (effective in 1900) was historically oriented, scientific, and professional. A large share of the credit (or blame) for the differences between the German and the French civil codes is owed to Friedrich Karl von Savigny, one of the most famous names in the history of the civil law tradition.

The idea of codification aroused widespread interest in Germany and other parts of Europe and in Latin America during the first part of the nineteenth century. The French code was widely admired and copied, and in the course of time it was proposed that Germany follow France's lead. However, Savigny and his followers—influenced by Kant, Hegel, and German Romanticism—opposed this effort, persuasively arguing a thesis that became very influential in Germany. Proponents of what came to be known as the historical school, these scholars maintained that it would be wrong for Germany to attempt to devise a civil code by reasoning from principles of secular natural law. In their view, the law of a people was a historically determined organic product of that people's development, an expression of the *Volksgeist*. Consequently, a thorough study of the existing German law and of its historical development was a necessary prelude to proper codification. Since the Roman civil law as interpreted by the medieval Italian scholars had been formally received in Germany some centuries before, a thorough historical study of German law had to include Roman law and old Germanic law as well as more recent elements of the contemporary German legal system. Under the influence of Savigny and the historical school, many German scholars turned their energies to the intensive study of legal history.

31

Savigny's idea was that by thoroughly studying the Roman law that was received in Germany and the German legal system in its historical context legal scholars would be able to draw from it a set of historically verified and essential principles. These features of the law could then be individually studied, studied in relation to other such principles, and eventually systematically restated. The result would be a reconstruction of the German legal system according to its inherent principles and features. This, in turn, would provide the necessary basis for the codification of German law.

The components of the German legal system, in their historical context, came to be thought of by certain successors of Savigny as something like natural data. Just as natural data in biology, chemistry, or physics could be studied to determine the more general principles of which they were specific manifestations, so the data of German law could be studied to identify and extract from them those inherent principles of the German legal order of which they were specific expressions. Hence the proposed reconstruction of the German legal system was to be a *scientific* reconstruction. (This concept is discussed at greater length in Chapter X.) Finally, the Germans were convinced that it was neither desirable nor possible to rid the world of lawyers. They expressly rejected the idea that the law be clearly and simply stated so that it could be correctly understood and applied by the popular reader. The German view was that lawyers would be needed, that they would engage in interpreting and applying the law, and that the code they prepared should be responsive to the needs of those trained in the law.

Consequently, the German Civil Code of 1896 is the opposite of revolutionary. It was not intended to abolish prior law and substitute a new legal system; on the contrary, the idea was to codify those principles of German law that would emerge from careful historical study of the German legal system. Instead of trying to discover true principles of law from assumptions about human nature, as the French did under the influence of secular natural law, the Germans sought to find fundamental principles of German law by scientific study of the data of German law: the existing German legal system in historical context. Rather than a textbook for citizens, the German civil code was thought of as a tool to be used primarily by professionals of the law.

Does this mean that the German civil code and the French civil code are totally dissimilar? It does not. There are differences, and they are important, but some overriding similarities remain. The

Germans, like the French, have incorporated a sharp separation of powers into their system of law and government. It is the function of the legislator to make law, and the judge must be prevented from doing so. While displaying a more sophisticated awareness of the difficulty of making a code complete, coherent, and clear, the Germans nevertheless sought to do exactly that, and for the same basic reasons that motivated the French. The German code also served a unifying function, providing a single body of law for the recently unified nation. And like the French code, it thus supported the emergence of the monolithic nation-state.

An entirely different set of ideals and assumptions is associated with the California Civil Code, or with the Uniform Commercial Code as adopted in any American jurisdiction. Even though such codes may look very much like a French or German code, they are not based on the same ideology, and they do not express anything like the same cultural reality. Where such codes exist, they make no pretense of completeness. The judge is not compelled to find a basis for deciding a given case within the code. Usually, moreover, such codes are not rejections of the past; they purport not to abolish all prior law in their field, but rather to perfect it and, except where it conflicts with their specific present purposes, to supplement it. Where some provision of a code or other statute appears to be in possible conflict with a deeply rooted rule of the common law, the tendency is to interpret the code provision in such a way as to evade the conflict. "Statutes in derogation of the common law," according to a famous judicial quotation, "are strictly construed."

Thus, the conservative tendencies of the common law tradition stand in marked contrast to the ideology of revolution from which the spirit of civil law codification emerged. It is this ideology, rather than the form of codification, that helps to bind civil law nations together in a common legal tradition. Like the work of the glossators and commentators, which was received together with the *Corpus Juris Civilis* in Europe, the ideas of European publicists and scholars of the eighteenth and nineteenth centuries have been adopted, together with the form of European codification, in the civil law nations of Latin America, Asia, and Africa. This work, and the ideology it embodies, is of prime importance to an understanding of the civil law tradition, as the following chapters demonstrate. We begin with the civil law image of judges.

33

VI

JUDGES

WE IN the common law world know what judges are. They are culture heroes, even parental figures. Many of the great names of the common law are those of judges: Coke, Mansfield, Marshall, Story, Holmes, Brandeis, Cardozo. We know that our legal tradition was originally created and has grown and developed in the hands of judges, reasoning closely from case to case and building a body of law that binds subsequent judges, through the doctrine of stare decisis, to decide similar cases similarly. We know that there is an abundance of legislation in force, and we recognize that there is a legislative function. But to us the common law means the law created and molded by the judges, and we still think (often quite inaccurately) of legislation as serving a kind of supplementary function. We are accustomed, in the common law world, to judicial review of administrative action, and in the United States to the power of judges to hold legislation invalid if unconstitutional is accepted without serious question. We know that our judges exercise very broad interpretative powers, even where the applicable statute or administrative action is found to be legally valid. We do not like to use such dramatic phrases as "judicial supremacy," but when pushed to it, we admit that this is a fair description of the common law system, particularly in the United States.

We also know where our judges come from. We know that they attend law school and then have successful careers either in private practice or in government, frequently as district attorneys. They are appointed or elected to judicial positions on the basis of a variety of factors, including success in practice, their reputation among their fellow lawyers, and political influence. Appointment or election to the bench comes as a kind of crowning achievement relatively late in life. It is a form of recognition that brings respect and prestige. Judges are well paid, and if they are among the higher judicial echelons, they will have secretaries and research assistants. If they sit on the highest court of a state or are high in the federal judiciary, their name may be a household word. Their opinions will be discussed in

34

the newspapers and dissected and criticized in the legal periodicals. They are very important people.

This is what common lawyers mean when they talk about judges. But in the civil law world, judges are something entirely different. They are civil servants, functionaries. Although there are important variations, the general pattern is as follows. A judicial career is one of several possibilities open to students graduating from university law school. Shortly after graduation, if they wish to follow a judicial career, they will take a state examination for aspirants to the judiciary and, if successful, will be appointed as a junior judge. (In France and several other nations, they must first attend a special school for judges.) Before very long, they will actually be sitting as judges somewhere low in the hierarchy of courts. In time, they will rise in the judiciary at a rate dependent on some combination of demonstrated ability and seniority. They will receive salary increases according to preestablished schedules and will belong to an organization of judges that has the improvement of judicial salaries, working conditions, and tenure as a principal objective.

Lateral entry into the judiciary is rare. Although the provision is made in some civil law jurisdictions for the appointment of distinguished practicing attorneys or professors to high courts (particularly to the special constitutional courts established since World War II), the great majority of judicial offices, even at the highest level, are filled from within the ranks of the professional judiciary. Judges of the high courts receive, and deserve, public respect, but it is the kind of public respect earned and received by persons in high places elsewhere in the civil service.

One of the principal reasons for the quite different status of civil law judges is the existence of a different judicial tradition in the civil law, beginning in Roman times. The judges (*iudex*) of Rome were not a prominent people of the law. Before the Imperial period they were, in effect, laypeople discharging an arbitral function by presiding over the settlement of disputes according to formulae supplied by another official, the praetor. The *iudex* was not expert in the law and had very limited power. For legal advice the judge turned to the jurisconsult. Later, during the Imperial period, the adjudication of disputes fell more and more into the hands of public officials who were also learned in the law, but by that time their principal function was clearly understood to be that of applying the emperor's will. Judges had no inherent lawmaking power. They were less limited in medieval and prerevolutionary times, when it was not unusual for Continental judges to act much like their English counterparts. That, indeed, was the problem: they were interpreting creatively, building a common law that was a rival to the law of the central government in Paris and even developing their own doctrine of stare decisis.

With the revolution, and its consecration of the dogma of strict separation of powers, the judicial function was emphatically restricted. The revolutionary insistence that law be made only by a representative legislature meant that law could not be made, either directly or indirectly, by judges. One expression of this attitude was the requirement that judges use only "the law" in deciding a case, and this meant, as we saw in Chapter IV, that they could not base their decisions on prior judicial decisions. The doctrine of stare decisis was rejected. An extreme expression of the dogma of strict separation of the legislative and judicial powers was the notion that judges should not interpret incomplete, conflicting, or unclear legislation. They should always refer such questions to the legislature for authoritative interpretation. It was expected that there would not be very many such situations, and that after a fairly brief period almost all the problems would be corrected and further resort to the legislature for interpretation would be unnecessary. (The history of the retreat from this position is described in the next chapter.)

The picture of the judicial process that emerges is one of fairly routine activity; the judge becomes a kind of expert clerk. Presented with fact situations to which a ready legislative response will be readily found in all except the extraordinary case, the judge's function is merely to find the right legislative provision, couple it with the fact situation, and bless the solution that is more or less automatically produced from the union. The whole process of judicial decision is made to fit into the formal syllogism of scholastic logic. The major premise is in the statute, the facts of the case furnish the minor premise, and the conclusion inevitably follows. In the uncommon case in which some more sophisticated intellectual work is demanded of the judge, he or she is expected to follow carefully drawn directions about the limits of interpretation.

The net image is of judges as operators of a machine designed and built by legislators. The judicial function is a mechanical one. In the past, the great names of the civil law were not those of judges (who knows the name of a civil law judge?) but those of legislators

(Justinian, Napoleon, Andrés Bello) and scholars (Gaius, Irnerius, Bartolus, Mancini, Domat, Pothier, Savigny, and a host of other nineteenth- and twentieth-century European and Latin American scholars). Civil law judges are not culture heroes or parental figures, as they often are with us. Their image is that of a civil servant who performs important but essentially uncreative functions.

It is a logical, if not a necessary, consequence of the quite different status of civil law judges that they are not widely known, even among lawyers. Their judicial opinions are not read in order to study their individual ways of thinking and their apparent preconceptions and biases. Although there are exceptions, the tendency is for the decisions of higher courts in civil law jurisdictions to be strongly collegial in nature. They are announced as the decision of the court, without enumeration of votes pro and con among the judges. In most jurisdictions separate concurring opinions and dissenting opinions are not written or published, nor are dissenting votes noted. The tendency is to think of the court as a faceless unit. (As we will see later, there are recent changes in this matter.)

The result is that, although there is a superficial similarity of function between the civil law judge and the common law judge, there are substantial disparities in their accepted roles. In part the contemporary civil law judge inherits a status and serves a set of functions determined by a tradition going back to the *iudex* of Roman times. This tradition, in which the judge has never been conceived of as playing a very creative part, was reinforced by the antijudicial ideology of the European revolution and the logical consequences of a rationalistic doctrine of strict separation of powers. The civil law judge thus plays a substantially more modest role than the judge in the common law tradition, and the system of selection and tenure of civil law judges is consistent with this quite different status of the judicial profession.

The establishment of rigid constitutions and the institution of judicial review of the constitutionality of legislation in some civil law jurisdictions has to some extent modified the traditional image of the civil law judge. In some jurisdictions (e.g., Austria, Italy, Germany, Colombia, Guatemala, Spain), special constitutional courts have been established. These special courts, which are not part of the ordinary judicial system and are not operated by members of the ordinary judiciary, were established in response to the civil law tradition that judges (i.e., ordinary judges—the modern successors

Judges

of the Roman *iudex* and the civil judges of the *jus commune*) cannot be given such power. With the establishment of these special courts run by specially selected judges, tradition is, at least in form, observed. Indeed, a few purists within the civil law tradition suggest that it is wrong to call such constitutional courts "courts" and their members "judges." Because judges cannot make law, the reasoning goes, and because the power to hold statutes illegal is a form of lawmaking, these officials obviously cannot be judges and these institutions cannot be courts. For many legal scholars, the increase of their power was considered undemocratic But even where, as in some nations in Latin America, the power of judicial review resides in the highest ordinary courts, the traditional civil law image of the judge retains much of its power. Judicial service is a bureaucratic career; the judge is a functionary, a civil servant; the judicial function is narrow, mechanical, and uncreative.

It is clear, however, that the traditional image of the civil law judge is waning. The trend is toward increased judicial scope and power. In France, the Conseil d'État, a quasi-judicial governmental organ, has been responsible for the development of administrative law. The members of the council are not called judges; instead, they use the old names of *conseillers d'État, maîtres de requêtes,* and *auditeurs.* Nevertheless, they are recognized as judges and adjudicate. There is no code of administrative law, nor has the legislation had the most important role in the development of administrative law. More generally, in most civil law jurisdictions an ordinary judge can reject the application of a statute if he or she considers it contrary to the constitution. In other jurisdictions, the judge has to refer the matter to a constitutional tribunal. The actions of national executives, legislatures, and judges can be reviewed by the constitutional judges and by judges of new supranational courts, like the European Court of Justice, the European Court of Human Rights, and the Inter-American Court of Human Rights. Some constitutional courts, like the German, the Spanish, or Colombian courts, and the Costa Rican Constitutional Chamber, have power and national prestige comparable to that of the Supreme Court of the United States. In Spain, Italy, and Colombia, among other countries, scholars and the media speak of judicial protagonism. The political science literature on judges of the civil law tradition is a rapidly expanding field. This trend is analyzed in the final chapters of this book.

VII

THE INTERPRETATION OF STATUTES

IT HAS been shown in earlier chapters that the doctrine of separation of powers, when carried to an extreme, led to the conclusion
that courts should be denied any interpretive function and should
be required to refer problems of statutory interpretation to the legislature itself for solution. The legislature would then provide an
authoritative interpretation to guide the judge. In this way defects
in the law would be cured, courts would be prevented from making
law, and the state would be safe from the threat of judicial tyranny.
To the civil law fundamentalist, authoritative interpretation by the
lawmaker was the only permissible kind of interpretation.

The nearest approach to that ideal to be found in the modern history of a major nation is the attempt of Frederick the Great, toward
the end of the eighteenth century, to make the law of Prussia judge-
proof. Under Frederick, Prussia adopted a code containing more
than 17,000 articles; by comparison, the Code Napoléon contains
2,281 articles. The Prussian code was an attempt to provide a specific, detailed solution for specific, detailed fact situations; the end
sought was a complete catalog of such solutions, available to judges
for any case that might come before them. At the same time, judges
were forbidden to interpret the code. In case of doubt, they were
to refer the question to the special Statutes Commission, which
had been created for that purpose. If they were caught interpreting, judges would incur Frederick's "very great displeasure" and be
severely punished. German legal historians tell us that the Statutes
Commission never played the role Frederick intended for it; that
the code, detailed as it was, did not provide obvious answers for all
cases; and that the judges perforce interpreted its provisions in their
daily work. Frederick's code, his commission, and his prohibition of
judicial interpretation are all considered failures.

The development of French *cassation* (from *casser*, meaning "to
quash") is the next logical, as well as chronological, step. The defects
and inconveniences of total reliance on authoritative interpretation
were apparent to practical lawyers in revolutionary France. They

knew that the legislature would find itself flooded with difficult, often seemingly trivial, requests for interpretation and that it would find the work of responding to such requests tiresome. The legislature was faced, however, with a theoretical dilemma: it might wish to avoid having to decide a constant stream of questions from the courts, but it could not allow the courts themselves to do the interpreting without undermining the doctrine of the separation of powers.

The solution chosen was, under the circumstances, perfectly understandable. A new governmental organ was created by the legislature and given the power to quash the courts' incorrect interpretations. In the legislative debates and in the law that was eventually promulgated, it was made clear that the new organ was not a part of the judicial system but rather a special instrument created by the legislature to protect legislative supremacy from judicial usurpation. Although it looked and acted very much like a court, the legislature preserved appearances by calling it the Tribunal (rather than Court) of Cassation and describing it as *auprès du corps legislative*, an expression that suggests an organ of the legislative body. The requirements of the separation of powers were met; legislative supremacy was upheld. Ordinary judges were to be kept from interpreting the statutes, and the legislature did not have to do such work.

It will be noted that the Tribunal of Cassation was not itself expected to provide authoritative interpretations of the statutes involved in the cases that came before it. On the contrary, its original function, consistent with its separate, nonjudicial nature, was merely to quash judicial decisions based on incorrect interpretations of statutes. Such cases would then go back to the judiciary for reconsideration and decision; that was, after all, a judicial function. Unlike the typical action of an appellate court in the United States, which not only quashes the incorrect decision of a question of law by the lower court but also indicates the proper answer to the legal question incorrectly decided below and, when appropriate, applies that result to the case to produce a new decision, the French Tribunal of Cassation was created to perform only the first of these steps. However, by a gradual, but apparently inevitable, process of evolution, the tribunal came to perform the second step as well as the first. Thus, it not only indicated that the judicial decision was wrong; it also explained what the correct interpretation of the statute was. During this same period, the tribunal's nonjudicial origin dropped from view, and it came to be called the Court of Cassation; thus judicialized, it assumed a position at the apex of the system of ordinary courts. In France, as well as in Italy and other nations that have followed the French model, the full title is likely to be Supreme Court of Cassation. Thus, the highest civil and criminal court in the jurisdiction—one that is staffed by judges and that has primary responsibility for assuring the correct and uniform interpretation and application of the statutes by the lower civil and criminal courts—is the direct descendant of a legislative tribunal originally created to keep the power of interpretation out of the hands of judges.

The final step in the evolution of such bodies is illustrated by the German institution of "revision," as distinguished from the French cassation. The French system stopped at the second step: the Supreme Court of Cassation could quash a decision based on an incorrect interpretation, and it could instruct the lower court as to the correct interpretation. Still, the case had to be sent back to the lower court ("remanded") for decision. This was often a mere formality that unnecessarily took up valuable time; and occasionally more serious problems arose because lower judges were either unable or unwilling to understand and follow the interpretation announced by the Supreme Court of Cassation. Nor were they, in theory, required to follow the higher court's decision. We have seen that judges had to base their decision on the law, and the opinions of the Supreme Court of Cassation were not, and still today they are not, a formal source of law. Thus, the decision of the Court of Cassation is at most something that is persuasive for its reasoning and the eminence of its source. But if the judge on remand is convinced that the law is otherwise, he or she should so hold. Much of the history of the process of cassation since the court's creation is the chronicle of such problems and of the various devices that have been invented to solve them. By the time Germany was united under Bismarck, the defects of French cassation were clearly apparent. And by that time European legal thought had openly conceded that judges did, indeed, have to interpret statutes as part of their ordinary work. There was no reason to complicate matters unnecessarily, so the Germans did the rational thing: they created a supreme court with the power to review the decisions of lower courts for legal correctness, to quash incorrect decisions, to indicate the correct answer, and to "revise" the incorrect decision accordingly.

The evolution from the argument for compulsory referral to the legislature for interpretation, through referral to a legislative tribunal, to emergence of a court with the power to review and correct interpretations by lower courts has necessarily been accompanied by a gradual acceptance of a power of interpretation by the ordinary judiciary. This evolution has also been accompanied by an enormous amount of discussion and writing, some of it to justify interpretation of statutes by courts, some of it to define the limits of the interpretative power, and some of it to specify how that power should be exercised. The mass of scholarship on interpretation in civil law countries (which is roughly analogous to the mass of literature in the United States on the judicial process) thus is in part an expression of uneasiness over the fact that courts are interpreting statutes and in part an expression of anxiety that they will abuse their power of interpretation; only a small proportion of it focuses on the actual process of interpretation. Many writers have sought to prove that judicial interpretation is not really in conflict with legislative supremacy and a strict separation of powers. Those interested in defining the limits of interpretation have been concerned with certainty in the law and the prevention of judicial tyranny and irresponsibility. Only a few writers have tried to give the judge help in facing up to particular problems of interpretation.

As we have seen, revolutionary ideology assumed that systematic legislation would be clear, complete, and coherent, reducing the function of the judge to one of merely applying the law (i.e., the statute) to the facts. This simplistic view of the judicial process, which has an amazing power of survival in the public mind and among some lawyers, is the precise equivalent of a simplistic attitude toward the work of judges in the common law world. Many laypeople among us, and even some lawyers, persist in believing that courts are bound by prior decisions and that the process of finding and applying the precedent to the case should be relatively mechanical. There is a folklore of the judicial process at work in both the common law and the civil law traditions.

Actually, it is extremely unlikely that thoughtful Continental jurists ever had much confidence in such a vision of the legal process. During the period of revolutions, it might have seemed important to act as though the revolutionary ideology was valid, but it is inconceivable that many legal scholars ever believed in it. It is too obvious that the facts are sharply different from the ideology. For one thing, the illusion of the self-applying statute, the legislative norm so clear that its application is an automatic process, was long ago dispelled by exposure to the facts. Ever since the revolutionary period, civil law courts have been engaged in hearing and deciding disputes whose resolution depends on the meaning to be given to a legislative provision. Such litigation is frequently appealed, and reversals of lower court decisions are far from uncommon. Hardly an article in a typical civil code has escaped the need for judicial interpretation to supply a meaning that was unclear to the parties, to their counsel, or to the judges themselves.

Likewise the dogma that a code can be complete and coherent fails to survive even a cursory glance at the jurisprudence (the civil law term for the set of judicial decisions). The books are full of decisions in which the court has had to fill gaps in the legislative scheme and reconcile apparently conflicting statutes. Although the text of a statute remains unchanged, its meaning and application often change in response to social pressures, and new problems arise that are not even touched on by any existing legislation. The ideal of certainty in the law becomes unattainable in the face of the uncertainty that exists in fact, where determination of the rights of parties frequently must await the results of litigation. Judges are not, in practice, relieved by clear, complete, coherent, prescient legislation from the necessity of interpreting and applying statutes. Like common law judges, they are engaged in a vital, complex, and difficult process. They must apply statutes that are seldom, if ever, clear in the context of the case, however clear they may seem to be in the abstract. They must fill gaps and resolve conflicts in the legislative scheme. They must adapt the law to changing conditions. The code is not self-evident in application, particularly to the thoughtful judge.

Despite these facts, the folklore of judicial interpretation has had surprising persistence in the civil law world. As a result, there is a tension between fact and folklore, and a substantial literature attempting to resolve that tension has grown up. Until recently the principal effort in that literature has been to try to preserve the folklore by explaining away the facts. Typically that literature approaches the topic under three headings: (1) the problem of interpretation in the strict sense (i.e., the unclear provision), (2) the problem of lacunae (i.e., nonexistent provisions); and (3) the problem of so-called evolutive interpretation (i.e., the statute whose meaning changes while its terms remain constant).

Each of these is a problem because of the requirement that the judge decide the case. Judges are not allowed to say that the law is unclear and therefore dismiss the action. The problem of interpretation in the strict sense then becomes one of justifying a decision by the judge when the legislative direction is unclear. This both makes the judge the lawmaker for the case and exposes the parties to the risk of judicial irresponsibility and arbitrariness. It is even worse in the case of lacunae, where the legislature has failed to provide any rule. Here the judge clearly is legislating for the case, and the dangers are even more apparent. And where, by judicial interpretation, a statute comes to mean something different from what it meant at the time it was enacted, the role of judge as lawmaker seems obvious.

The orthodox civil law response to the problems of interpretation is well illustrated in the provision of the Italian Civil Code of 1942 dealing with the interpretation of statutes:

In interpreting the statute, no other meaning can be attributed to it than that made clear by the actual significance of the words according to the connections between them, and by the intention of the legislature.

If a controversy cannot be decided by a precise provision, consideration is given to provisions that regulate similar cases or analogous matters; if the case still remains in doubt, it is decided according to general principles of the legal order of the State.

The first paragraph of this statute (which has itself been subject to a great deal of interpretation by Italian courts, producing a substantial body of interpretation about interpretation) is the legislative direction to the courts on the problem of interpretation in the strict sense. The statute should be applied according to its plain meaning, and if that is unclear, the judge should look to the intention of the legislature in enacting the statute. Obviously, such directions to the judge say either too much or too little. If it is clear what is meant by the statute, then there is no problem. If it is not clear what is meant, "the actual significance of the words" is a mirage. Words have no inherent significance; they are supplied with meaning by those who use them, and the problem before the judge is to supply meaning when it is not clear what the legislators meant when they used the words. The resort to legislative intent may be helpful in some cases, but reconstruction of the historical process of forming and expressing intent in a forum as complex as a representative legislature is a very risky enterprise. In a surprising number of cases, the legislative history will show that the legislature did not foresee the problem facing the judge and consequently had no intent concerning it. Indeed, it is generally agreed among scholars that the search should be not for the actual legislative intent, but for the "intention, spirit, objective content of the norm [i.e., statute] itself." Such admonitions as those contained in the first paragraph of the Italian statute, and similar admonitions to judges in other civil law countries, consequently do not help judges solve the problem of the unclear statute. They merely establish conceptual sets consistent with the orthodox view of judicial interpretation and tell judges that they must articulate their results in those terms. Judges are not told how to decide; they are told how to state what they have decided.

The second paragraph of the statute is the direction to the judge regarding the problem of lacunae. If there is no statutory provision bearing precisely on the point, the judge is to reason by analogy from other statutory provisions. If this does not work, then the judge is to resort to something called "general principles of the legal order of the State," a provision that has emerged from many years of ideological debate. The analogous reference in the Austrian Civil Code of 1811 was to "the principles of natural law." That provision represented the general view prevailing before the ultimate victory of state positivism. The idea was that there was something called natural law existing apart from the positive law of any form of government and flowing from the nature of humankind and the natural requirements of order in society. During this period, the principal debate was between different schools of natural law—in particular, between the secular and the Roman Catholic schools. Later in the nineteenth century the word "natural" was dropped from the usual formulations. This was clearly a step away from natural law and toward unchallenged state positivism, but it was not far enough away to still the debate. The formulation in the Italian statute quoted earlier has quieted all doubts in Italy. The tendency in other civil law jurisdictions is also away from any reference to or reliance on natural law. As to the actual significance of the instructions concerning resolution of the problem of lacunae, we must wait until Chapter X and the discussion of legal science. There it will be shown that this sort of instruction to the judge is useful mainly as a means of reconciling the folklore of judicial interpretation with the dominant school of legal thought in the civil law world.

The most difficult problem of interpretation to solve in a manner consistent with legislative supremacy and the separation of powers is that of evolutive interpretation. The phenomenon is familiar enough: an old statute, if applied in the traditional way, will produce a clearly undesirable result in the case before the judge. It is not that the prior interpretation was wrong; often it will have been confirmed by a judgment of the Supreme Court of Cassation (or its equivalent). But circumstances may have changed sufficiently to require a different interpretation in the present case. The problem for judges is that if they decide according to the old interpretation, the result of the case will be offensive to themselves, to the parties, and to society. If they reinterpret the statute to achieve a result satisfactory to themselves, to the parties (at least one of them), and to society, they will be making law. They could defer to the legislature and refuse to reinterpret the statute, calling on the legislature to change the law to meet modern requirements. However, this would not give much satisfaction to the parties in the case, and it would make impossible demands on the legislature. In most civil law jurisdictions this would be denial of justice: a judge's grave fault. Consequently, there is general agreement in civil law jurisdictions that judges do have the power to interpret evolutively. The discussion thus shifts from the legitimacy of this function to the question of its justification and its proper limits. Predictably, the traditional scholarship on this problem of interpretation is concerned primarily with proving that the judge, in interpreting evolutively, does not really make law.

Much of the writing on the topic of judicial interpretation in the civil law world is, as has been already suggested, designed to prove the continuing validity of the folklore of judicial interpretation, and this view is still taught to law students by many professors. More recently, there have been a variety of reactions against the folklore. Such schools of thought as the jurisprudence of interests, sociological jurisprudence, and legal realism, among others, have their partisans. In Switzerland, the civil code instructs judges that when all aids to interpretation fail, they should employ the rule they would adopt if they were a legislator. In these and many other ways, the folklore of judicial interpretation is losing ground. Nonetheless, many still believe in it, and those who do not cannot ignore it; they must refute it. The folklore of judicial interpretation is a characteristic part of the civil law tradition.

As noted earlier, judicial decisions are not a source of law. It would violate the rules against judicial lawmaking if decisions of courts were to be binding on subsequent courts. The orthodox view consequently is that no court is bound by the decision of any other court in a civil law jurisdiction. In theory, at least, even though the highest court has already spoken on the question and indicated a clear view of its proper resolution, the lowest court in the jurisdiction can decide differently.

This is the theory, but the facts are different. Although there is no formal rule of stare decisis, the practice is for judges to be influenced by prior decisions. Judicial decisions are regularly published in most civil law jurisdictions. A lawyer preparing a case searches for cases in point and uses them in argument; and the judge deciding a case often refers to prior cases. Whatever the ideology of the revolution may say about the value of precedent, the fact is that courts do not act very differently toward reported decisions in civil law jurisdictions than do courts in the United States. Judges may refer to a precedent because they are impressed by the authority of the prior court, because they are persuaded by its reasoning, because they are too lazy to think the problem through themselves, because they do not want to risk reversal on appeal, or for a variety of other reasons. These are the principal reasons for the use of authority in the common law tradition, and the absence of any formal rule of stare decisis is relatively unimportant. Those who contrast the civil law and the common law traditions by a supposed nonuse of judicial authority in the former and a binding doctrine of precedent in the latter exaggerate on both sides. Everybody knows that civil law courts do use precedents. Everybody knows that common law courts distinguish cases they do not want to follow, and sometimes overrule their own decisions.

Even though these facts are obvious and widely known, the folklore persists. Otherwise thoughtful civil lawyers frequently ignore the widespread use of precedent by their own courts, just as equally thoughtful common lawyers frequently oversimplify and misrepresent the use of precedent by common law courts. The important distinction between the civil law and the common law judicial processes lies not in what courts in fact do but in what the dominant folklore tells them they do. In the orthodox civil law tradition, the judge is assigned a comparatively minor, inglorious role as a mere operator of a machine designed and built by scholars and legislators. We now turn to an examination of the way this judicial image is reflected in the peculiar emphasis on certainty in the civil law and in the denial of inherent equitable power to civil law judges.

VIII

CERTAINTY AND EQUITY

THERE IS a great emphasis in the literature of the civil law tradition on the importance of certainty in the law. Certainty is, of course, an objective in all legal systems, but in the civil law tradition it has come to be a kind of supreme value, an unquestioned dogma, a fundamental goal. Even though most civil lawyers would recognize that there are competing values whose preservation might require some sacrifice of certainty, the matter is usually not discussed in these terms. In the civil law world it is always a good argument against a proposed change in the legal process that it will impair the certainty of the law. In Italy under Mussolini, for example, some attempts of the Fascists to make the law into an instrument of the totalitarian state were successfully resisted by jurists in the name of certainty in the law. After the fall of Fascism and the establishment of the republic, many desirable reforms in the Italian legal system were resisted by other jurists, again in the interests of certainty. Certainty is an abstract legal value. Like a queen in chess, it can move in any direction. Nevertheless, certainty generally favors the protection of property and freedom. It has gained new strength in present-day promotion of rule of law.

Although the ideal of certainty has been used for a variety of purposes, its most important application is a reflection of the distrust of judges and administrators. In the interest of certainty judges are prohibited from making law and legislation should be clear, complete, and coherent. The process of interpretation and application of the law should be as automatic as possible, again in the interest of certainty. In this sense, the emphasis on certainty is an expression of a desire to make the law judge-proof, to place limits on the discretion of administrators, and to oblige legislators to be clear and respect fundamental rights.

Legal certainty is also recognized as desirable in the common law tradition, but there are three major differences. First, certainty is usually discussed in more functional terms and is not elevated to the level of dogma. It is recognized that people should, to the extent possible, know the nature of their rights and obligations and be able to plan their actions with some confidence about the legal consequences, but it is also widely recognized that there are limits on the extent to which certainty is possible. Second, certainty is achieved in the common law by giving the force of law to judicial decisions, something theoretically forbidden in civil law. The accumulation of judicial decisions in the course of time in a jurisdiction provides a variety of concrete, detailed examples of legal rules in operation. These, together with the statements of the rules themselves, are likely to provide more certainty about the law than are bare legislative statements of the rules. Thus, the desire for certainty is an argument in favor of stare decisis in the common law tradition, whereas it is an argument against stare decisis in the civil law tradition. Finally, in the common law world (particularly in the United States) it is more generally recognized that certainty is only one of a number of legal values, which sometimes conflict with each other. Certainty frequently implies rigidity; law that is certain may be difficult to mold in response to changed circumstances or to bend to the requirements of a particular case. In the common law, certainty and flexibility are considered competing values, each tending to limit the other. In the civil law world, the supreme value is certainty, and the need for flexibility is viewed as a series of "problems" complicating progress toward the ideal of clear legislative rules. Hence the concern described in the preceding chapter about interpretation by judges is frequently put in these terms: if judges are not carefully controlled in the way they interpret legislation, then the law will be rendered more uncertain. The same general attitude exists toward equity. In its general sense, equity refers to the power of the judge to mitigate the harshness of strict application of a statute, or to allocate property or responsibility according to the facts of the individual case. Equity is, in other words, a limited grant of power to the court to apply principles of fairness in resolving a dispute being tried before it. It is a recognition that broad rules, such as those commonly encountered in statutes, occasionally work harshly or inadequately, and that some problems are so complex that it is not possible for the legislature to dictate the consequences of all possible permutations of the facts. Where such problems are involved, it is thought better to leave the matter to the trier of the case, to decide according to equitable principles. Equity thus is the justice of the individual case. It clearly implies a grant of discretionary power to the judge.

But in the civil law tradition, to give discretionary power to the judge threatens the certainty of the law. As a matter of legal theory, judges have no *inherent* equitable power. They may from time to time be granted authority to use equity in the disposition of a case, but that grant of power will be expressly made and carefully circumscribed in a statute enacted by the legislature. Although the matter has produced much discussion in the past and is still the source of argument among civil law scholars, the dominant view is still that, in the interest of certainty, judges must be carefully restricted in the exercise of equity.

The civil law has, then, sacrificed flexibility for certainty. In contrast, the common law tends to strike the balance between them more equally. Some of the reasons for this difference in attitudes toward judicial discretion in the two legal traditions have already been described in the preceding two chapters. There is, however, an additional cause: the existence in England for several centuries of a separate system of chancery courts and a separate body of legal principles called equity.

The Norman conquerors of England at the Battle of Hastings quickly set about centralizing the government, including the administration of justice. They established royal courts and a system of royal justice that gradually displaced the old feudal courts and rules. In the process of centralizing English justice, the judges of the royal courts developed new procedures and remedies and a new body of substantive law applicable, at least in theory, to all English people. For this reason it was called the common law. The common law, at first dynamic and creative, eventually developed into a rigid, circumscribed set of procedures and remedies applied according to inflexible, technical rules. The common law became bound by formulas and rules. However, individuals who were dissatisfied with the remedy available to them in the royal courts, or who wished to complain about the fairness of a decision, could always petition the king for relief. The king had the power to vary the operation of his system of justice on the basis of such petitions (a power that has a vestigial equivalent today in the power of a chief executive to pardon and commute).

From time to time the king himself may have considered and acted on such petitions, but before long the task was delegated to a royal official, called the chancellor. This official (often known as "the king's conscience") was given the power to vary the operation of the law in the interests of fairness. There were, of course, many complaints about actual or fancied abuses of this discretionary power and about the uncertainty it involved; at one time there was a popular saying to the effect that justice was measured by the length of the chancellor's foot. But as the process of hearing and acting on petitions for relief from the law became more institutionalized and formalized, and as the volume of business became sufficiently great to require assistants to help the chancellor decide, the discretionary grant of relief from the operation of the law became more and more judicialized. Formalities, rules of procedure, and substantive rules were developed to govern the submission of petitions to the chancellor and his action on them. By gradual degrees the chancellor became a court of chancery, and the rules applied in chancery proceedings became a separate body of law, called equity, in recognition of the court of chancery's historical origins.

So, for several centuries two separate systems of justice existed in England: the law courts and the common law on one side, and the chancery courts and equity on the other side. In general, during their separate existence the jurisdiction of the chancery court was limited to ameliorating the harsh operation of some aspects of the common law and supplying remedies in cases where the common law remedy was considered inadequate. Eventually the separate systems of courts and of law and equity were abolished, and the jurisdictions and principles merged. The surviving common law tradition consequently consists of both the original common law and the tempering influence of equity.

A comparative law scholar has remarked that the civil law today is what the common law would look like if there had never been a court of chancery in England. Historically this statement requires nuances. Precodification judges in the civil law tradition paid very little attention to legislation, and as we will see later, the generality of codes gave considerable leeway to judges. But belief and attitudes are important: two specific contributions of equity to the common law tradition help explain the differences between the contemporary common law and civil law traditions. These are judicial discretion and the civil contempt power.

As to judicial discretion, common law judges traditionally have inherent equitable powers: they can mold the result in the case to the requirements of the facts, bend the rule where necessary to achieve substantial justice, and interpret and reinterpret to make the law respond to social change. These powers are not seen as threats to certainty in law; indeed, certainty is to be achieved through the doctrine of stare decisis, itself a judicial doctrine. The difficulties of rationalizing the demand for certainty and the justice of the individual case thus become problems for solution by the judges themselves. There is no conflict on this question between the judicial and the legislative powers of government. In the common law judges can exercise discretion, but they also must bear the major operational responsibility for certainty and stability in the law.

Hence common law judges, as compared to their civil law counterparts, are less compelled by prevailing attitudes to cram the dispute into a box built by the legislature. Even when the case involves application of a statute, common law judges have some measure of power to adjust the rule to the facts. If the box supplied by the legislature does not fit, judges can make minor adjustments in it to make it fit. Where the applicable law is precedent, a box built by one or more prior judges, this power is even greater. In the civil law world, on the contrary, if the facts do not fit the box, they must be forced out of shape in order to make them fit. And the box is, in theory, always built by the legislature.

It is one thing to say that the civil law judge lacks inherent equitable power. That statement is true. It is quite another matter to accuse the civil law of being less equitable than the common law. That statement is demonstrably false. Indeed, a good argument can be (and has been) made that the civil law has developed a better, because more equitable, body of substantive rules in some fields of law than has the Anglo-American system. Our concern here is not with relative fairness but with the distribution of power between legislature and court. In the common law tradition the judge has inherent equitable power. In the civil law tradition that power does not exist. The way in which the legislature acts, and the resulting effect on the judiciary, provides an excellent example of the contrast between the theory and the practice of the legal process in the civil law tradition.

The theory is that the legislature exercises its equitable power in either of two principal ways: it can specifically delegate that power, in carefully defined situations, to the judge, or it can itself enact rules of equity for the judge to apply like other rules. An example of the first type is found in Article 1226 of the Italian civil code, which tells the judge that if the precise amount of the damage to the plaintiff resulting from a breach of the defendant's obligation cannot be proved, the judge shall fix the amount according to equitable principles. An example of the second type is found in Article 1337 of the same code, which provides that the parties to a contract shall act in good faith in the negotiation and formation of the contract. Any modern civil code anywhere in the civil law world will contain a number of such provisions.

It requires no great exercise of imagination to realize that the second type of statute transfers a large segment of undefined equitable power to the judge. It is true that the legislature has acted and that its action is expressed as a substantive rule of law, but the terms are so broad ("good faith," which is not defined in the code, has an almost unlimited area of potential application) that the judge is hardly constrained by the legislative formulation. What that statute means depends on what judges do with it in concrete cases. What they do with it in concrete cases becomes the law in fact, although not in theory. A lawyer who wants to learn what effect to anticipate from the application of that statute will turn immediately to reported decisions in which it has been applied by courts. The legislature has not provided the box; it has, in effect, told the judges to make the box themselves.

The practice of delegating power to courts through legislation that employs general clauses of this sort is a common one in the civil law world, although the extent to which judges have consciously exercised that power varies widely. Article 1382 of the Code Napoléon provides that one whose act injures another must compensate that person for the injury. The French courts have built an entire body of tort law on the basis of that article. Article 242 of the German Bürgerliches Gesetzbuch (BGB) requires a person to perform his or her obligation in the manner required by good faith. The German courts have employed this statute to create an immense body of new law on the performance of obligations. Both sets of courts have, in the process, developed working attitudes toward case law that are much more like those of common law courts than the prevailing theory admits. The German courts have been particularly overt about it, and their reliance on Article 242 to deal with some of the problems arising out of Germany's disastrous post–World War I inflation provides an example of judicial activism that seems extreme even to hardened legal realists. The obligatory reference to a "source of law" in such decisions is an empty ritual that has little restraining effect on judges and, given the rejection of stare decisis, can hardly contribute much to certainty.

At the same time, the compliance of German judges with the wishes of the Nazi regime is often unfavorably compared with the more successful resistance of Italian judges to the Fascists. The German judges, so the argument goes, had aggressively opted for judicial discretion at the expense of certainty in the 1920s, both to justify their use of general clauses and to follow the theory advanced by the "free law" school of jurists. The Italian judges stayed with their traditional approach of emphasizing certainty and exercising only a very limited degree of discretion. When darkness fell, the German judges were unable to defend the legal order by calling on the importance of certainty. Unlike the Italians, they had openly abandoned that principle. Whether or not one is persuaded by this version of history is unimportant. The fact that many do believe it gives us some insight into the continuing vitality of the appeal to certainty and the continuing distrust of judicial discretion that one finds in even the most liberated of civil law nations.

A second major distinguishing contribution of equity to the common law tradition is the civil contempt power. This is the power of a court in a civil (i.e., noncriminal) case to punish a person who violates a court order by ordering the person to perform or to refrain from performing an act. The idea is that the court can order people to do something or not to do something and punish them if they disobey the order. The contempt power is used for a wide variety of purposes in the common law. People living near an airport who are annoyed by airplanes flying too low over their property may get an injunction against further flights below a certain altitude. If the injunction is disobeyed, the offender can be punished by the court. One who has promised to convey some land to another but subsequently refuses to do so may be ordered to do so by a court, and if the person refuses, he or she can be punished for the refusal. A labor group illegally picketing an employer can be enjoined from continuing to picket, and the responsible officials of the union can be punished if the picketing does not stop. The variety of situations in which such orders addressed to individuals are employed as a remedy in the common law is very great. The power behind these orders is the power of the court to punish individuals for failing to obey them—the contempt power.

There is no civil contempt power in the civil law tradition. A general power to address orders to specific persons and to punish them for failure to follow the orders is unknown. The French do have something they call the *astreinte*, which appears, in a limited way, to be a functional equivalent of the contempt power; and something like the *astreinte* can also be found in German law. The French *astreinte*, in particular, has recently been expanded by legislation, but it is still only a pale imitation of the broad power of the common law judge. In the early twentieth century, Mexico developed the *amparo*, a special procedure for the protection of constitutional rights that has been exported to other Latin American countries, sometimes with different names (*mandado de segurança* in Brazil, *tutela* in Colombia, *amparo* in Venezuela and in Central American countries). The *amparo* is a powerful injunction enforceable by contempt power, and judges in Latin America are increasingly using it.

The very idea of giving a court the general power to compel individuals in civil actions to do or to refrain from doing certain acts under penalty of imprisonment or fine—or both—is foreign to the civil law tradition. For one thing, it is inconsistent with the demand for certainty; it gives the judge a great deal more power than civil lawyers think judges ought to have. In addition, fines and imprisonment for refusal to obey orders sound to civil law jurists more like criminal than civil penalties. Accordingly, the view is that the substantive and procedural safeguards incorporated in criminal law and criminal procedure are usually necessary before the imposition of penalties on individuals. Such safeguards do not exist in noncriminal law. Finally, the civil contempt power does not seem necessary to the administration of justice in the civil law tradition. The assumption is that individuals' property will answer for their obligations. The power of the civil court is usually limited to the giving of money judgments, based on express statutory authorization, in all but one class of cases. In the exceptional situation, the civil court may order the doing of an act, but only where the act is one that can be performed by a third person—a so-called fungible act. The cost of the performance can then be charged to the defendant, and, if necessary, the appropriate legal significance can be given to the act by the judge. For example, where one who has the legal obligation to do so but does not execute the instrument needed to convey land, the court may have the appropriate instrument prepared and may give it the necessary legal effect.

The different emphasis on certainty, and the presence or absence of inherent judicial discretion and the contempt power, thus exemplifies the fundamental differences in the roles of the judiciary in the two legal traditions. These two things reveal the extent to which the civil law judge is still limited by a variety of historical influences, most prominently by the image of the judicial process that emerged in the period of the French Revolution and by the refinement of that image that took place under the impact of legal science, to which we turn next. But before we enter this new subject, it will be good to remark that the civil law tradition evolves, just as all traditions. It is clear that judges have more power nowadays and that no one today would deny the importance of decisions of the constitutional courts, the supreme courts, the courts of cassation, and the international courts. Lawyers reference judicial decisions in their arguments, and legal scholars include them in their writings or directly comment on them. The critical point is that even if the rule of stare decisis has not been formally adopted, mention of judges' decisions is growing and is often justified as improving legal certainty. Certainty is the chess queen.

The dispute over whether common law and civil law judges decide differently is probably impossible to resolve, but there is no doubt that they have different understanding of the "sources of law" and that they formulate and support decisions in different ways. If lawyers wish to be persuasive, they have to be aware of the types of arguments they should use in each legal culture.

IX

SCHOLARS AND LEGAL EDUCATION

WE HAVE seen that the role of the civil law judge is generally thought to be much more restricted and modest than that of the common law judge. It is reasonable to speak of the common law as a law of the judges, but no one would think of using such terms in speaking of the civil law even if the world is changing. The alleged abuses perpetrated by judges under the old regime and the conception of the role of judges that emerged in France during the revolution converge to limit what judges are supposed to do. Legislative positivism, the dogma of the separation of powers, the ideology of codification, the attitude toward interpretation of statutes, the peculiar emphasis on certainty, the denial of inherent equitable power in the judge, and the rejection of the doctrine of stare decisis—all these tend to diminish the judge and to glorify the legislator.

From this, one might suppose that the protagonist of the legal process in the civil law tradition is the legislator. Indeed, it was hoped for a time that the legislature would produce bodies of law that were complete, coherent, and clear, so that interpretation would be unnecessary. The retreat from the dogma of legislative infallibility has been a slow, grudging one. Although it is now admitted that civil law courts have an interpretive function, the fiction is still maintained that in performing that function, the judge does not create law but merely seeks and follows the expressed or implied intent of the legislator. All this suggests that the civil law legislator occupies the dominant position held in the common law tradition by the judge. For brief periods in the history of the civil law tradition this may have been true, but the legislators soon found themselves again in the shadow of the people who were primarily responsible for the theory of the modern nation-state; for the doctrines of legislative positivism and the separation of powers; for the form, style, and content of codification; and for the dominant view of the nature of the judicial function. The teacher-scholar is the real protagonist of the civil law tradition. The civil law is a law of the professors.

By way of contrast, although the influence of law professors and legal scholarship may be growing in the United States, judges still exercise the most important influence in shaping the growth and development of the American legal system. Moreover, the prevailing ideology assumes that they play this role, and they themselves are conscious of what is expected of them. The tradition of the scholar as an important force in the development of the common law is very recent and still, comparatively, very weak. The common law is still a law of the judges.

The preeminence of the scholar in the civil law tradition is very old. The Roman jurisconsults—who advised the praetor and the judge, and were recognized as experts on the law but had no legislative or judicial responsibility—are considered the founders of this scholarly tradition. Their opinions had great weight, and during the second century the opinions of certain jurisconsults were binding on judges. Their opinions were written down, collected, and treated as authoritative. Much of the most important part of Justinian's *Corpus Juris Civilis*—especially the *Digest*—is made up of the work of jurisconsults.

After the revival of Roman law in Italy, those responsible for the revival and development of the medieval *jus commune* were scholars. Law professors at the universities wrote comments (glosses) on the *Digest* and also opinions on different legal and political problems. The work of the glossators and the commentators, added to Justinian's *Corpus Juris Civilis*, made up the body of Roman law received throughout Western Europe. During this period, their writings were in some places given binding authority in courts, a practice analogous to the use made of jurisconsults during the classical period of Roman law. For a time in Germany, for example, cases were frequently sent by courts to law faculties for decision. Many of the codes drafted in Europe and in Latin America during the nineteenth century were the work of scholars, and all were based on the writings of earlier generations of scholars. The great debate about codification in Germany was begun and conducted by scholars. In Italy, which is in many ways the archetypal civil law jurisdiction, several recent prime ministers and presidents have been professor-scholars of law.

It is instructive to reexamine the role of scholars in the two great legislative periods in the history of the civil law tradition—that of Justinian and that of codification in the nineteenth century. It will be recalled that Justinian was much concerned with the work of schol-

58

ars. The accumulated mass of writing about the law was, in his view, a source of unnecessary confusion and difficulty. He did not, however, propose to abolish the authority of all the jurisconsults. Instead, he wished to select from the existing mass of legal scholarship whatever was worthy of preservation. This was one of the assignments he gave to the commission appointed to compile the *Corpus Juris Civilis,* a commission composed entirely of scholars. The *Digest,* which is the largest and most important part of the *Corpus Juris Civilis,* is in large part a compilation of the work of Roman legal scholars. The Institutes, another part of the *Corpus Juris Civilis,* is based on a textbook on Roman law with the same title, written by Gaius, a law professor.

Even the French codification movement relied heavily on the work of scholars, although Napoleon himself took an active part in its preparation and enactment. The actual work of drafting the French codes was put into the hands of commissions composed of practicing lawyers and judges; but these commissions were dominated by the work of scholars (particularly that of Robert Pothier), and the changes made in their drafts by the legislature were merely minor variations within the commissioners' grand scholarly design. A large part of the ideology of French codification came from scholarly and philosophical sources, including the works of men like Puffendorf and Montesquieu. This ideology later dominated the interpretation and application of the codes in France and was adopted in civil law nations that drafted their codes on the lines of the French model, again under the influence of men of learning (e.g., the Latin American Andrés Bello, Teixeira da Freitas, and Vélez Sarsfield). The German codification, as we shall see, was even more thoroughly dominated by scholars.

Why, then, the curious ambivalence of the legislator toward the scholar? Why, for example, did Justinian forbid the preparation of commentaries on the *Corpus Juris Civilis?* One can only guess. His desire to restore the classical Roman law of an earlier, greater period may have been accompanied by the fear that commentaries prepared during his lifetime or at some subsequent time would be of a lower quality. Like much of the work excluded from the *Corpus Juris Civilis,* they would be inferior to the scholarship of the classical period. A second possibility is that Justinian thought that his compilation represented perfection, so that any commentary could only detract from its merit. Third, as emperor, Justinian saw the *Corpus Juris Civilis,* officially promulgated by him, as the reigning body of law for the empire and believed that commentaries on his legislation might tend to impair its authority. Justinian's prohibition against the publication of commentaries was, of course, ignored during his lifetime.

Although he did not attempt to forbid them, Napoleon hoped that no commentaries on his civil code would be published. This hope, like Justinian's command, was ineffectual. According to a well-worn story, his reaction when he was informed that the first commentary had been published was to exclaim, "My code is lost!" One reason for such a statement was the illusion that the code was so clear, complete, and coherent that commentaries on it were superfluous. Another was the fear that, once the code fell into the hands of legal scholars, its usefulness as a popular law book for French citizens would be diminished. Another may have been apprehension about the tendency of scholars to think in conservative, historical terms. Napoleon wanted his code to transcend the old regional divisions and to provide the basis for a completely new legal order. All prior law on topics covered by the code was repealed, but the new law had to be protected against interpretation according to prerevolutionary legal ideas to make that repeal effective.

Thus, both Justinian and Napoleon called on prominent jurists to carry out the very complicated task of drafting far-reaching legal reforms, but they feared the influence of scholars on their reforms. Other evidences of legislative distrust of legal scholarship frequently crop up in the civil law world. In contemporary Italy, for example, the legislature has told the courts that they may not cite books and articles in their opinions. Therefore, Italian judges, who are heavily influenced by legal scholarship, employ the ideas suggested to them by scholars without citing them, and refer in a very general way to "the doctrine," which is the civil law term for books and articles written by legal scholars. This easy circumvention of the Italian parliament's command is merely another example of the futility of legislative attempts to eliminate or even reduce the influence of the scholar in the civil law world. Despite legislative efforts to dam it, the great river of legal scholarship in the civil law tradition moves on, providing the ideology and the basic content of legislation and eventually engulfing it.

We begin to understand the true importance of the civil law scholar when we look at how lawyers are educated, the role of law professors in explicating the law and the nature of their scholarly publications. Historically, civil lawyers were educated at the university by law professors, and from the eighteenth century onward, the method was the professors' lectures. The systematic treatises of the school of natural and international law do not leave room for the discussion of cases or for discussion at all. They just have to be explained. The same happened when the law was codified and the codes occupied the center of teaching in the nineteenth century. The authority of the professor-lecturer (and frequently book author) is supreme. The legal science, originally a German innovation that was later adopted by other civil law jurisdictions, accentuated the systematic character of law and legal scholarship. In the twentieth century, shorter books (précis or manuals) gave systematic treatment to specific branches of the law and gradually replaced the old treatises. Across these changing forms, the literature produced by the professor-scholars tends to give the image of law as a well-organized system of norms.

A typical book on Continental legal history illustrates the important role of the civil law scholar. Much of what is called legal history in the civil law tradition is baffling to common lawyers who first approach it. They are used to thinking of legal history as an account of legal rules and institutions in their historical, economic, and social contexts. The legal history they read is full of great cases, occasional statutes, and historical events. But when they pick up a book on legal history in the civil law tradition, they are likely to find the bulk of it devoted to a discussion of schools of legal thought and of disputes between legal scholars and their followers. They will read about the glossators, the commentators, the humanists; about the differences among the French scholars of the eighteenth century; and about the debate between Savigny and Anton Thibaut on codification in Germany. All in all, it is a peculiar form of intellectual history, almost entirely divorced from socioeconomic history on the one hand, and from discussion of the origin and development of specific legal institutions on the other. The protagonist of this form of legal history is the legal scholar, and its subject matter is currents of thought about the structure and operation of the legal order.

This is what we mean when we say that legal scholars are the dominant actors of the civil law. Legislators, executives, administrators, judges, and lawyers all come under the scholars' influence. Scholars mold the civil law tradition and the formal materials of the law into a model of the legal system. They teach this model to law students and write about it in books and articles. Legislators and judges accept their ideas of what law is, and when legislators and judges make or apply law, they use concepts the scholars have developed. Thus, although legal scholarship is not a formal source of law, the doctrine carries immense authority.

In the United States, where the legislature is also theoretically supreme, there is a well-known saying (originated by a judge) that the law is what the judges say it is. This is, properly understood, a realistic statement of fact. Judges have to decide how to characterize legal problems presented to them, which principles of law to apply to the problems, and how to apply them in order to arrive at a result. Whether the principles they choose are embodied in legislation or in prior decisions, they achieve substantive meaning only in the context of a specific problem, and the meaning attributed to them in that context is necessarily the meaning supplied by the judges. In a similar sense, it is reasonably accurate to say that the law in a civil law jurisdiction is what the scholars say it is.

Of course, traditions are not immutable, and the civil law and common law traditions have had reciprocal influences. The historical differences between these traditions in patterns of legal education have diminished over time. The creation of the American law school was a nineteenth-century innovation in the common law world. It incorporated a central element of the civil law tradition: teaching law at the university to prepare lawyers for practice. This model has now been adopted in most common law countries, including England.

The American law school introduced two other innovations not usually found in the civil law tradition, the case method and graduate studies in law. American law schools have become simultaneously a place for high-quality scholarship and strong preparation for professional life. The American legal literature incorporated judicial decisions and, more recently, interdisciplinary literature in the discussion of cases. Many civil lawyers come to the United States (and more recently to England) to study law and become acquainted with the more interdisciplinary legal reasoning and educational approaches. Several of them have begun introducing the American style of legal education in their country of origin. In summary, scholarship and legal education are becoming a place of slowly convergence of the two traditions, but the feeling is that we are in a very early stage of this convergence.

X

LEGAL SCIENCE

IN CIVIL law jurisdictions, the way legal scholars look at the law is the way everyone looks at it. This was true in Bologna after the revival of Roman legal studies, where the dominant point of view about what law was and how it should be studied and taught was developed by the glossators. When one refers to the work of the glossators, one refers to their objectives, their methods, and their image of the legal process, as well as to their views on specific legal problems.

As the influence of the glossators waned, a new group of scholars, the commentators, gained ascendancy. The view of the law held by glossators and commentators, and their method of studying and teaching law, came to be called the Italian style (*mos italicus*). The commentators and the Italian style were succeeded by the humanists and the French style (*mos gallicus*), and later by the school of natural and international law. At any given moment in the history of the civil law tradition a number of different points of view will be in competition with each other, but one or another will always tend to dominate. The contemporary civil law world is still under the sway of one of the most powerful and coherent schools of thought in the history of the civil law tradition. We will call it legal science. It is the fifth component of the civil law tradition (after Roman civil law, canon law, commercial law, and the legacy of the revolutionary period) and the final one to be discussed in this book (although in Chapter XX we will speculate about a nascent sixth subtradition).

Legal science is primarily the creation of German legal scholars of the middle and late nineteenth century, and it evolved naturally out of the ideas of Savigny. As explained in Chapter IV, Savigny argued that German codification should not follow the rationalist and secular natural law thinking that characterized the French codification. He maintained that a satisfactory legal system had to be based on the principles of law that had historically been in force in Germany. Therefore, a necessary preliminary step to codification was a thorough study of the legal order to identify and properly state these principles and to arrange them in a coherent system.

Because private law, and particularly that part of it we have called Roman civil law, was thought to be the heart of the legal system, the German scholars put their principal efforts into study and restatement of the principles of Roman civil law as received in Germany and as modified by the addition of Germanic elements. They concentrated their study on the *Digest* (in German *Pandekten*, from the Latin *Pandectae*) of Justinian, and thus came to be called the Pandectists. They produced highly systematic treatises based on principles they drew from their study of Roman law. The *Digest* had been studied thoroughly for centuries, but the mid-nineteenth-century Germans brought this study to its highest and most systematic level. Their work culminated in the publication of influential treatises and, impelled by the unification of Germany under Bismarck in 1871, in the promulgation of the German Civil Code of 1896 (the BGB). The treatises and the BGB were influential throughout the civil law world (and also, to some extent, in the common law world, where there was a flurry of enthusiasm for legal science). The methods and the concepts developed by the German scholars were applied to other fields of law, both private and public, and hence came to dominate legal scholarship. Despite a variety of criticisms and reactions against it from the time of Savigny to the present, legal science continues to affect the thinking of civil law scholars, and hence of other legal actors, in the civil law tradition.

The concept of legal science rests on the assumption that the materials of the law (e.g., statutes, regulations, customary rules) can be seen as naturally occurring phenomena, or data, from whose study the legal scientist can discover inherent principles and relationships, just as the physical scientist discovers natural laws from the study of physical data. As a leading German scholar of the time, Rudolph Sohm, put it: "The scientific process, by means of which principles are discovered that are not immediately contained in the sources of law, may be compared to the analytical methods of chemistry." Under the influence of this kind of thinking, legal scholars deliberately and conscientiously sought to emulate natural scientists. They intended to employ the scientific method, and they sought admission to the community of scientists. (It should be added that similar assumptions, but with less emphasis on science and the scientific method, underlay some of the work of legal scholars in the United States in the late nineteenth century and constituted one source of justification for the famous case method of teaching in American law schools).

Like the natural sciences, legal science is highly systematic. Principles derived from a scientific study of legal data are made to fit together in a very intricate way. As new principles are discovered, they must be fully integrated into the system. If new data do not fit, either the system must be modified to accommodate them, or they must be modified to fit the system. In this way the preservation of systematic values becomes an important consideration in criticizing and reforming the law.

This emphasis on systematic values tends to produce a great deal of interest in definitions and classifications. Much scholarly effort has gone into the development and refinement of definitions of concepts and classes, which are then taught in a fairly mechanical, uncritical way. The assumption of legal science that it scientifically derives concepts and classes from the study of natural legal data on the one hand, and the generally authoritarian and uncritical nature of the process of legal education on the other, tend to produce the attitude that definitions of concepts and classes express scientific truth. A definition is not seen as something conventional, valid only so long as it is useful; it becomes a truth, the embodiment of reality. Serious arguments are conducted about the "autonomy" of certain fields of law, such as commercial law or agrarian law, or about the "true" nature of specific legal institutions. Law is divided into clearly delimited fields. Public law and private law, as is explained more fully in the next chapter, are treated as inherently different and clearly distinguishable. There is a precisely defined legal vocabulary and an accepted classification of law that are reflected in the curricula of the law schools, in the professorial chairs in the faculties of law, in the arrangement of books in law libraries, in the subject matter of works written by legal scholars, and in the approach of legislators to lawmaking.

The order thus imposed on the legal system by legal science represents a great systematic achievement. Civil lawyers are justly proud of their legal structure and methodology and of the very real contribution it makes to the certain, orderly, and efficient statement, elaboration, and administration of the law. Every phase of the legal process is a beneficiary of this systematic jurisprudence, and the absence of anything equivalent to it in the common law is one of the reasons civil lawyers think of the common law as crude and undeveloped.

Because the components of this systematic restatement of the law, although theoretically inherent in the existing positive legal order, did not exist there in identified, articulated form, and because the legal order was a universe of data within which inherent principles were to be identified, new concepts had to be invented to express these components and principles. The novelty of these concepts and their prominence in the work of scholars committed to legal science eventually led critics to call this kind of doctrine conceptual jurisprudence. Because communication without concepts is difficult, it hardly seems fair to criticize legal science for using them. What was peculiar to legal science was that its concepts were new (or were given a new emphasis), that the accent was on their "validity" rather than their functional utility, that their proper arrangement and manipulation were thought to be the province of scholars, and that they tended to be highly abstract.

This high level of abstraction—this tendency to make the facts recede—is one of the most striking characteristics of legal science to a lawyer from the United States or England. The principles developed by legal scientists have been taken out of their factual and historical context, and are consequently lacking in concreteness. Legal scientists are more interested in developing and elaborating a theoretical scientific structure than they are in solving concrete problems. They are on a quest for the ever more pervasive legal truth, and in the process of making statements more abstract, "accidental" details are dropped. The ultimate objective is a general theory of law from which all but the essential elements have been removed.

The work of legal science is carried on according to the methods of traditional formal logic. The scholar takes the raw materials of the law and, by an inductive process sometimes called logical expansion, reasons to higher levels and broader principles. These principles themselves reveal on further study the even broader principles of which they are only specific representations, and so on up the scale. The principles derived by logical expansion are, at one level, the "provisions that regulate similar cases or analogous matters" and, at a higher level, the "general principles of the legal order of the state" that judges should employ in dealing with the problem of lacunae in the interpretation of statutes (see Chapter VII). Intuition and the subconscious, despite their powerful influence on human affairs, are excluded from this process. The result is something that Max Weber called "logically formal rationality."

Finally, legal science attempts to be pure. Legal scientists deliberately focus their attention on pure legal phenomena and values, such as the "legal" value of certainty in the law, and exclude all others. Hence the data, insights, and theories of the social sciences, for example, are excluded as nonlegal. Even history is excluded as nonlegal—and this seems peculiarly inconsistent in view of the fact that Savigny and his disciples are called the historical school. It is of interest to historians (including legal historians) but not to legal science. Nor is the legal scientist interested in the ends of law, in such ultimate values as justice. These may properly be the concern of philosophers, including legal philosophers, but the legal scientist is concerned only with the law and with purely legal values. The result is a highly artificial body of doctrine that is deliberately insulated from what is going on outside, in the rest of the culture.

However, although legal scientists sought to be value-free and pure, they were ideological captives of their era. The creative work of the legal scientists took place in nineteenth-century Europe, in the intellectual climate that has since come to be called nineteenth-century European liberalism. Among the more relevant aspects of this ideology was a strong emphasis on individuals and their autonomy. Private property and liberty of contract were treated as fundamental institutions that should be limited as little as possible. It was an era of what we would now consider exaggerated individualism. The heart of the law was the Roman civil law, and the Roman civil law was basically a law of property and contract. Legal scientists concentrated their work in this area of civil law, and the body of doctrine they eventually produced embodied the assumptions and values central to the thought of their time. Under the banner of legal science they built ideologically loaded concepts into a systematic conceptual legal structure that is still taught in the universities' faculties of law; that limits and directs the thinking of the legal scholars who perpetuate it; that provides the parameters of judicial interpretation and application of laws, precedents, and legal transactions; and that, in a word, dominates the legal process. The role of these assumptions and values is concealed behind a façade of ideological neutrality, of the scientific study of purely legal phenomena. In this way European systematic jurisprudence embodies and perpetuates nineteenth-century liberalism, locking in a selected set of assumptions and values and locking out all others.

The special attitudes and assumptions about law that characterized the work of the Pandectists and that make up what is here called legal science can thus be summarized in the following terms: "scientism," "system building," "conceptualism," "abstraction," "formalism," and "purism." These characteristics of legal science are apparent to many civil lawyers, and there have been many reactions against it in the civil law world. These reactions have taken a variety of forms, and they seem to have been gathering force in the period since World War II; but legal science is far from dead. In all except the most advanced civil law jurisdictions, it reigns mostly undisturbed. It dominates the faculties of law, permeates the textbooks, and thus is self-perpetuating. Most law students are indoctrinated early in their careers and never think to question it: its characteristics, and the model of the legal system that it perpetuates, are all they know. Legal science has been subjected to direct attack and to subversion from many sides. Its critics have tried to introduce consideration of concrete problems, to see that the existence of a subconscious and of intuition are taken into account, to bring nonlegal materials to bear on the legal consideration of social problems, and to involve legal scholars in the conscious pursuit of socioeconomic objectives and the discussion of public policies. Nevertheless, most civil lawyers still form their own ideas of the law according to the teachings of legal science. Some of the consequences of these attitudes are described in subsequent chapters.

Although the common law world has seen occasional brief trends toward the kind of thinking that characterizes legal science, it has never really caught on here. Legal science is a creation of the professors—it smells of the lamp—and our judge-dominated law is fundamentally inhospitable to it. Common law judges are problem solvers rather than theoreticians, and the civil law emphasis on scientism, system building, formalism, and the like gets in the way of effective problem solving. It also diminishes the role of the judge in the legal process, to the advantage of the legislator and the scholar. Both sociological jurisprudence (which is the opposite of abstraction, formalism, and purism) and legal realism (which rejects scientism and system building) emphasize the difficulty and the importance of focusing on the judicial process. Both have flourished in the common law world, and particularly in the United States.

It is true that the famous case method of instruction, which is a creation of law professors in the United States, originated under the influence of German legal science; the idea was that decisions of courts, being sources of law, should be studied as data with the aim of deriving principles of law from them and finally arranging them into a coherent system. The end product of this line of thought in the United States was *The Restatement of the Law* (prepared mainly by professors), and its publication provided the occasion for a thorough, devastating attack by the legal realists. Since that attack, legal science has been essentially discredited in the United States, and the emphasis in legal education has subtly shifted. Cases are still studied, but they are no longer studied as the data of legal science. Instead, they are seen as convenient records of concrete social problems and as convenient examples of how the legal process operates.

The basic difference is epitomized in another quotation from the German legal scientist Rudolph Sohm, in the *Institutes of Roman Law*: "A rule of law may be worked out either by developing the consequences that it involves, or by developing the wider principles that it presupposes. . . . The more important of these two methods of procedure is the second, i.e., the method by which, from given rules of law, we ascertain the major premises they presuppose. . . . The law is thus enriched, and enriched by a purely scientific method." An American legal realist would resist the implication that rules of law should be the principal objects of study or the suggestion that there are only these two ways of studying them. But if pushed to Sohm's choice, most law professors, judges, and lawyers in the United States would easily and quickly choose the first of his two methods. Most civil lawyers would still choose the second. By the same token, sociology of law has been present in many countries of the civil law tradition from early twentieth century as a critical strand of formalism. This new strand has gained strength in the present time, as we will see in the last chapter of this book.

XI

THE GENERAL PART

THE ACCEPTED major classifications of law within the civil law tradition are public law and private law. Within private law there are two main fields: civil law and commercial law. Technically, the civil law (which is the modern descendant of Roman civil law) includes only the law of persons (natural and legal), the family, inheritance, property, and obligations. This is roughly the same subject matter as that covered in the Institutes of Justinian and the civil codes of the nineteenth century. The firm belief that these subjects, which seem quite disparate to a common lawyer, constitute a coherent body of interrelated legal principles and institutions is itself one of the distinguishing features of the civil law tradition. The principal operating legal concepts, the basic structure of the law, and the principal legal institutions are all directly drawn from or developed by analogy to the civil law. The apparatus of legal scholarship owes its origins to scholars of the civil law, and the systematic conceptual structure developed for this field has eventually been adapted to all the other fields. It is still generally believed that it is the function of the civil law scholar to develop general theories of law that are valid for the entire legal order. The growth of public law resulting from the vast increase in state activity in the past century has shaken this attitude but not displaced it. Civil law is still fundamental law. It is studied first, and subsequent study builds on it. It forms the matrix of thought of the lawyer in the civil law tradition.

In addition to the formal sources of the civil law, typically contained in a civil code and supplementary legislation, there is an overlay of concepts and principles derived primarily from legal scholarship. These concepts and principles and the system they form carry the great weight of scholarly authority described in Chapter IX. Although many of these concepts and principles have never existed as such in the positive civil law, they have been introduced into the legal order by scholars, under the influence of legal science, as general legal truths derived by the scientific method from the positive law.

This superstructure of derived concepts and principles typically appears in three distinct but closely related contexts in the civil law tradition: (1) the Allgemeiner Teil, or general part, of the German Civil Code of 1896 and other civil codes that follow the German pattern; (2) the set of basic notions on which scholars build extremely complex and sophisticated general theories of law; and (3) the content of the "introduction to law" that is taught to students at the beginning of their legal education. These three have tended to merge in those nations in which civil codes have been adopted or extensively revised under the impact of German legal science of the late nineteenth century. Even though such nations have not always copied the German Civil Code, there has been a strong tendency to make their own codes more "scientific." The extent to which evolution toward a scientific civil code has taken place thus determines the degree to which the positive law, the basic elements of accepted general theories of law, and the introductory or general part of courses and treatises on civil law employ the same concepts and principles. As a rule, the positive law is a good deal less scientific, in this sense, than the law taught and written by scholars.

The best way to capture some of the flavor of the general part of the civil law is to examine the general part of a more or less typical textbook for a civil law course. For this purpose we will sample the contents of the preliminary notions and general part of a respected elementary work (which shall remain anonymous) on private law. Although this work is not identical to similar books on French or German or Italian civil law, the pattern and the basic concepts are representative of the sort of thinking we are trying to describe.

The book begins with some "preliminary notions," the first of which is "the legal order." We are told that "no society . . . is able to live in an orderly way without an aggregate of rules governing the relations among the persons who compose the group (*ubi societas ibi ius*) and individuals who are charged with enforcing their observance." Applying this observation to the state, "we . . . establish the necessity both for an aggregate of norms that regulate the relations among citizens and for . . . organs and institutions that . . . enforce observance of the norms established by the state." [It will be observed that this definition of the legal order, limited to rules, or norms, and institutions for their enforcement, omits processes. This is a typical traditional approach. The legal order is seen as something static. Law is viewed not as a process for the perception and resolution of problems, but as a set of established rules and institutions. Instead of studying how such institutions perceive and resolve problems, or how they make, interpret, and apply the law, the doctrine focuses on the substantive content of the existing rules as its major object of study.]

The author begins his examination of the first component of the legal order in this way: "The legal norm . . . is . . . a command addressed to the individual by which a determined conduct . . . is imposed on him." [Actually, not all norms command; the text statement is inaccurate. There are many norms, particularly in the field of private law, that merely state the legal consequence of a state of fact; for example, if a person dies intestate, a certain proportion of his or her property passes to the person's children.] Many norms, including all those of private law, not only require or prohibit but also "correlatively attribute to another person a power." The debtor is told to pay the debt, and the creditor is given the power to obtain payment. Hence the distinction between objective law and subjective right. "Objective law is the rule to which the individual must make his conduct conform; subjective right is the power of the individual that is derived from the norm." Objective law can be distinguished into natural law and positive law. "Our study is directed exclusively toward positive law." [Here are two very significant and ideologically loaded fundamental notions. The first is that of the subjective right. In private law, this is the foundation of a legal system in which private, individual rights—that is, property, contract, personal, and family rights—exist. The second is the rejection of natural law, and hence of any normative system external to the state by which the validity of the positive law can be judged.]

The legal norm is more than mere advice; to the precept is joined a threat of "an evil administered by . . . the state" if it is not observed. The nature of this sanction distinguishes the legal norm from rules of custom, rules of etiquette, religious norms, and moral norms, whose nonobservance leads to other kinds of consequences (social disapproval, pangs of conscience). [This emphasis on sanctions is very misleading. Many legal norms bear no express or implied "threat of an evil administered by the state." It distorts legal reality to speak in such a way about rules of intestate succession to property, rules defining the different types of contract (e.g., sale, loan, lease), and rules stating which courts have jurisdiction to hear and decide what kinds of cases (e.g., civil or criminal, large or small claims), to select only three examples.] The legal norm is also general; its command is addressed not to specific individuals but to a model "fact situation": the debtor who does not pay is liable for damages. If a concrete fact corresponds to this model—for example, Smith does not pay his debt to Jones—then the effects established by the norm follow; that is, Smith is liable to Jones for damages. [The reader will recognize that the traditional view of the judicial function described earlier is implicit in this statement. Once the facts of the case are found, the judge compares them with the model fact situations in the legal norms, selects the norm whose model corresponds to the facts of the case, and applies the consequence stated in that norm.] One difficulty with the model fact situation is that occasionally the application of the abstract norm to the concrete case "gives place to consequences that offend the sense of justice." Equity is the power to vary application of the norm; it is "the justice of the individual case." But "the legal order frequently sacrifices the justice of the individual case to the demands of certainty in the law, inasmuch as it is believed that subjecting the legal order to the subjective valuation of the judge is dangerous; it is better that individuals know in advance the precepts they must observe and the consequences of nonobservance (the principle of certainty of law)." [See the discussion of certainty in Chapter VIII.]

These "preliminary notions" having been described, the author now moves to "the general part" of the civil law. He first distinguishes public law from private law: "The first governs the organization of the state and the other public entities . . . and the relations between them and the citizen, relations in which the state and the public entities are in a position of supremacy with respect to the citizen, who is . . . in a state of subjection and subordination. . . The private law regulates the relations among citizens. . . A characteristic of private law, in contrast to public law, is thus equality of position among subjects." [Compare the discussion of the public law–private law dichotomy in Chapter XIV.] At this point the discussion turns exclusively to private law. The author points out that private law norms are either dispositive or imperative. "The first can be modified by private arrangements or agreements; the second, insofar as they refer to the protection of fundamental social interests, are not subject to modification by individuals."

Next comes a discussion of the sources of law (i.e., of legal norms), which are said to be statutes, regulations, and custom, in that order.

[See Chapter IV.] This is followed by a discussion of the temporal effect of legal norms: rules for determining when statutes shall take effect, methods of abrogation, the rule against retroactivity, and the effect of a change in a statute on partly completed or continuing states of fact. Then the author discusses interpretation of the legal norm [see Chapter VII], ending with a brief discussion of "the conflict of laws in space," which shows how to determine what legal norms apply when those of two or more nations are possibly applicable.

The author then turns from the legal norm to the legal relation. "Human relations can be of various kinds: they can be inspired by affection, by sentiment, by friendship, by interest, by conviviality, by cultural interests, etc. Everyone instinctively grasps the difference between those relations and that which exists between me and my debtor. This relation is regulated by the law, which attributes to me the power (subjective right) to obtain payment of the debt, and puts on my debtor the obligation to pay. Thus the legal relation is the relation between two subjects regulated by law. When one wishes to allude to the persons who have put a legal relation into effect (for example, a contract), one uses the expression *parties.* Opposed to the concept of parties is that of third persons. The third person is, in general, one not a party and not subject to a legal relation. It is a general rule that the legal relation does not produce effects either in favor of or against third persons (*res inter alios acta tertio neque prodest, neque nocet*)." [This rule is subject to so many exceptions that its usefulness is questionable; actually there are many situations in which the private legal relation does affect the legal interests of third persons. The tendency in the general part to overstate general propositions and to submerge exceptions is here clearly illustrated. Leaving aside the inaccuracy of the generalization, note that there is no reference to the very interesting question of whether, and if so under what circumstances, third persons *should* be affected by private legal relations. The tenets of traditional scholarship—particularly the belief that only legal considerations, narrowly defined, are of interest to the legal scholar—exclude these matters from discussion. The rule is stated as the product of scientific investigation. No normative judgment on it is expressly made, but the methods and objectives of legal science and the authority of the doctrine give it a normative impact. In terms of the "is" and the "ought," the statement in question misstates the "is," avoids discussing the "ought," and implies a normative judgment that the misstated "is" is the desirable rule.]

In general, the term "subjective right" is used to indicate the legal interest of the person who has the benefit of a legal relation in private law. "The ultimate end that the norm seeks is always the protection of general interests. In many cases, however (and it is the rule in private law), it is the view that the best way to pursue this end consists in promoting individual interests, in stimulating individual initiative. The legal order recognizes the interests of the individual and seeks to effect the realization of his intention. Therefore the subjective right is defined as the primacy of intention, as the power to act for the satisfaction of one's own interests, protected by the legal order." [Here again we encounter the fundamental importance of the subjective right in private law. In addition, the reference to "the primacy of intention" conceals a long, voluminous scholarly debate. Some argued that private rights could be created, and private obligations imposed, only with the conscious assent of the individuals concerned. They were seeking the ultimate source of private legal relations, and they found it in the individual intention, or will. The *Willenstheorie* and the rule, criticized earlier, concerning the effects of legal relations on third persons, are logically related to each other. If the will or volition of the individual is taken as the true source of the legal obligation, then it seems right to conclude that one who has not expressed the will or volition to enter into the relation— that is, one who is not a party to it—cannot be subjected to the obligation and cannot claim the benefits of it. (The parties to the contract are bound by it only because they voluntarily entered into the contract.) But if the *Willenstheorie* is abandoned, and if the view is generally taken that the true source of the rights and obligations arising out of the legal relation is the positive legal order itself, then the third persons rule does not necessarily, or even logically, follow. Instead, one is freer to adopt a more eclectic approach to the problem of whether and under which circumstances third persons should be legally affected by the agreement of the parties to the legal relation. The author does not discuss the point.]

The holder of a subjective right is not required to compensate others for any prejudice that the exercise of the right may cause to them, except where he abuses the right. [The criticisms made previously of the rule that third persons are unaffected by a private legal relation apply to one interpretation of this statement. If it means anything, it is far from accurate, and it embodies a set of value judgments that the author never discusses. Is it true that the holder of the right is free to exercise it to the injury of others, so long as he does not "abuse" the privilege? Why? In addition, we could argue that the statement is nothing more than a tautology. If we say that the holder of a subjective right is liable to others for the exercise of that right only if he abuses it, then we have said that he is not liable for exercise of the right except when he is liable for the exercise of the right.] In some jurisdictions, such as France, courts use a general doctrine of scholarly origin to define "abuse of right." In others it is thought dangerous "to entrust the determination of the limits of the subjective right to the discretionary and variable criteria employed by judges." In the interests of certainty, then, the judge has this power only in selected, legislatively defined cases. [Observe the repeated emphasis on certainty in connection with the concern about giving discretionary power to judges, as described in Chapter VIII.]

"The first and fundamental division of subjective rights" is into "*absolute rights,* which guarantee to the owner a power that he can exercise against all others (*erga omnes*), and *relative rights,* which give him a power that he can exercise only against one or more determined persons. Typical absolute rights are the *real rights,* that is to say, rights in a thing. These attribute sovereignty, either full (ownership) or limited (real right in another's thing), over a thing to the owner. The immediate relation between the person and the thing stands out clearly, and is effective without need for the cooperation of others. Other subjects must merely abstain from interfering in the peaceful exercise of this sovereignty. In an obligatory relation, however [where only relative rights are involved], the conduct of another subject who is held to a determined conduct is of primary importance. The category of relative rights coincides with that of *rights of credit* (which are also called *personal rights* in contrast to real rights); that of the absolute rights includes not only the real rights but also the so-called rights of personality (right to a name, to one's image, and so on). The reverse, whether of the right of credit or of the real right, is the *duty:* negative duty of abstention in the real right, and duty (more precisely, *obligation*) of one or more determined persons in the right of credit."

He continues: "The legal relation is constituted when the subject acquires the subjective right. Acquisition indicates the association of a right with a person, who then becomes its owner: in substance, a subjective right becomes a part of the person's patrimony. The acquisition can be of two kinds: by *original title,* when the subjective right arises in favor of a person without being transmitted from another; and by *derivative title,* when the right is transmitted from one person to another. In acquisition by derivative title, one observes this phenomenon: the right that appertains to one person 'passes to another. This phenomenon is called *succession.* It indicates a change in the subject of a legal relation. In acquisition by derivative title, the new subject has the same right that the preceding titleholder had, or a right derived from it. This justifies the following rules: (1) The new titleholder cannot exercise a right greater than the one the preceding titleholder had (*nemo plus iuris quam ipse habet transferre potest*); (2) The validity and efficacy of the new title depend as a rule on the validity and efficacy of the preceding title." [Here again, these "rules" are subject to so many qualifications and exceptions that their usefulness as rules is dubious. In any legal system, there are cases in which the transferee of a right may get more or less than the transferor had, and the validity and efficacy of the new title can depend on factors other than the validity and efficacy of the preceding title. And as is often the case, these "rules" embody normative judgments about a variety of undisclosed issues.]

The author next turns to "the subject of the legal relation," discussing the legal characteristics of physical persons and legal persons (e.g., companies, foundations). Then, under the heading "the object of the legal relation," he discusses the legal concept of a thing (corporeal and incorporeal, movable and immovable, fungible and nonfungible, divisible and indivisible, consumable and nonconsumable, and so on).

Having discussed the basic characteristics of the legal relation in private law, typified by the subjective right and the subjective duty, the author turns to the proudest achievement of the civil law doctrine: the "juridical act." [This is the archetypal product of the methods and objectives of legal science discussed in Chapter X. Whole libraries of books and articles have been written on it. In some nations the notion has been employed in legislation (e.g., in the German Civil Code, where it is called the *Rechtsgeschäft*). In others it is found only in the doctrine. But in any civil law nation it functions in two major ways: as a central concept in the systematic reconstruction of the legal order produced and perpetuated by scholars and, together with the concept of the subjective right, as the vehicle for assertion and perpetuation of the role of individual autonomy in the law.]

The concept of the juridical act is based on another concept, the "legal fact." Recall that the legal norm contains a statement of a

model fact situation and a legal result. If the concrete facts that fit
the model fact situation occur, then the legal result becomes operative. A legal fact is an event (e.g., birth or death of a person, a
contract) that fits a model fact situation and therefore has certain
legal consequences. It is a legally relevant fact, as distinguished from
those that have no legal relevance. Legal facts include "natural facts
that come into being without the participation of our intention (the
death of a person from sickness, an earthquake), as well as acts deliberately and voluntarily performed by men." Thus the distinction of
legal facts into two categories: legal fact in the strict sense (i.e., mere
legal fact) and deliberate, voluntary legal acts.

"Legal acts are distinguished into two large categories: acts that
conform to the requirements of the legal order (*licit acts*) and acts
that are performed in violation of legal duties and that produce injury
to the subjective right of others (*illicit acts*). The licit acts are subdi-
vided into *operations,* which consist of modifications of the external
world (for example, the taking of possession, the construction of a
ship), and *declarations,* which are acts directed toward communicat-
ing one's thought, one's state of mind, or one's intention to others.
The acts intended to communicate one's thought or one's state of
mind are called *declarations of knowledge* (for example, notification);
the acts intended to communicate one's intention constitute *juridical acts.* These last have been the object of significant doctrinal elaboration; as to the others, which are also called *legal acts in the strict
sense,* the single point of certainty seems to be the nonapplicability
of principles relative to the juridical act. In general, one can say that
legal acts in the strict sense are acts that presuppose intention and
deliberation in the actor, but not the intention to produce a legal
effect: this is attached automatically by the legal order to the performance of the act. For example, if a person declares in writing in an
unequivocal manner that he is the father of a child conceived out of
wedlock, the child has a right to support according to the civil code,
even if the declarer did not have any intention to attribute such a
right to him by the act of declaration.

"Among legal acts, the juridical act is of fundamental importance.
In fact, it constitutes the most complete and interesting expression
of legal activity. To understand the notion of the juridical act well, it
is desirable to move to an empirical demonstration. He who executes
a will or the parties who enter into a contract intend to produce
legal effects: to distribute one's goods among the persons that the

testator will leave at the moment of his death or to transfer by sale the ownership of a thing in exchange for the price, and so forth. It is easy, therefore, to understand the definition given by the prevailing doctrine: the juridical act is a declaration of intention directed toward legal effects that the legal order recognizes and guarantees. And it is this direction of the intention toward legal effects that constitutes the characteristic element of the concept of the juridical act, and distinguishes it from legal acts in the strict sense, which—as we have seen—are also voluntary and deliberate acts, but produce their effects without requiring that the intention of the person who performs them be directed toward the production of these specified effects. These legal effects at which the parties aim are recognized and guaranteed by the legal order: this distinguishes the juridical act from illicit acts, which—as we have seen—violate duties established by the legal order. The juridical act is a general figure elaborated by the writers drawing on the study of particular legal figures (contracts, wills, and so on). These figures present common characteristics. The fundamental characteristic consists in the fact that these are expressions of private autonomy, of the power that the legal order recognizes in individuals to regulate their own interests. This power is not, however, unlimited: the liberty of the subject to put transactions into being is subordinated to observance of rules dictated by the order, which establishes a series of burdens and limits. (For example, if one wishes to transfer real property, it is necessary to use the written form.) Above all, it is required that the purpose to which the act is directed be recognized as worthy of protection by the legal order. The study of the general theory of the juridical act is very important. Because the legal order recognizes the power of the will of individuals in regulating their own interests in the field of private law, the greater part of legal activity consists of juridical acts."

[The preceding paragraph illustrates several characteristics of legal science: the emphasis placed in the traditional doctrine on "private" juridical acts and the "private" legal relations arising out of them; the empirical stance of the doctrine ("the juridical act is a general figure elaborated by the writers drawing upon the study of particular legal figures"); and the remoteness of the doctrine from concrete problems. How, for example, does one go about determining whether a specific act is or should be considered "worthy of protection by the legal order"? Who decides, and by what criteria? How does the legal process function to place this kind of limit on private autonomy?]

Next follows a description of the various types of juridical acts (unilateral or multilateral, inter vivos or at death, gratuitous or onerous, and so on). Then the author begins an extensive discussion of the elements of the juridical act. "The elements of the juridical act are divided into *essential elements*, without which the act is void, and *accidental elements*, which the parties are free to include or not. The essential elements are called *general* if they apply to every type of act (e.g., intention, cause); *particular* if they refer to the particular type being considered. Thus in a sale, besides intention and cause, the thing and the price are essential." Then follow discussions of the general essential elements (intention and cause) and of the general accidental elements (condition, time limit, mode). And finally come discussions of interpretation and effects, and of the consequences of voidness and voidability of the juridical act.

The general part of this manual then closes with brief general discussions of the judicial protection of subjective rights and the proof of legal facts in civil actions. The general part is contained in 236 pages—more than a fourth of the entire volume. More than a hundred of those pages deal with the juridical act. Nowhere in the general part is there a discussion of specific subjective rights or specific legal institutions. The progress is from the more general and abstract to the less general but still abstract. The discussion of specific subjective rights and specific legal institutions later in the volume goes on within the conceptual structure established in the general part. More important, the later discussion has the same tone and style; the emphasis is on inclusive definitions, clean conceptual distinctions, and broad general rules. There is no testing of definitions, distinctions, and rules against reality. Indeed, the tone set trains the lawyer to make the concrete facts fit into the conceptual structure. The tendency is to preserve the rule from the exception, to smooth out the rough spots.

The law of the general part is thus doctrinal law; it is a law purely of the scholars, and if we encounter it in the enacted, living law of a civil law nation, as in Germany, it is because the lawmaker has chosen to put the doctrine into statutory form. The civil codes that preceded the German BGB naturally contain no similar general part, but even those that followed it have, on the whole, preferred to maintain a formal separation between the scientific work of the scholar and the lawmaking work of the legislator. The result, in most modern civil codes, is that the legislation reflects but does not expressly embody the general doctrinal scheme here described. However, it is enacted, interpreted, and applied by people whose minds have been trained in the doctrinal pattern and to whom the scheme here described seems basic, obvious, and true. The conceptual structure and its inherent, unstated assumptions about law and the legal process constitute a kind of classroom law that hovers over the legal order, deeply affecting the way lawyers, legislators, administrators, and judges think and work.

Attempts to introduce a similar systematic reconstruction of the basic elements of positive law in the common law world have, on the whole, been failures. There was a time, toward the end of the nineteenth century, when legal scholars in England and the United States sought to emulate German legal science. The introduction of the case method of instruction in the Harvard Law School during the 1870s was based partly on the assumptions of legal science. Early in the twentieth century English and American analytical jurists produced a good deal of scholarship that resembles the work of legal science in a number of ways, and from time to time there are revivals of interest in analytical jurisprudence in the common law world. The ambitious undertaking called *The Restatement of the Law*, begun in the 1920s and carried on by a group of outstanding professors at major American law schools, has had much in common with the civil law doctrine typified by the discussion of the general part described in this chapter. But there have also been a number of counterinfluences: the impact of sociological jurisprudence and of legal realism, the lesser role of legal scholars and their work, the dominance of the problem-solving judge, and the different style and objectives of American legal education are among them. Most thoughtful legal scholars in the United States and England recognize the value of order and system, and they long, at least occasionally, for the introduction of a similar degree of order into our law. At the same time, most of them believe that the price is likely to be too high. They fear that this kind of order costs more in terms of sensitivity to the needs of a highly complex, constantly changing society than people should be willing to pay. Even those who are willing to pay that price lack the power within the legal process that is needed to establish a doctrinal system. They are teacher-scholars, and the protagonist of our legal process is still the judge.

XII

THE LEGAL PROCESS

IN THIS chapter we discuss who does what in the legal system and why; we want to try to understand the basic division of labor in the legal process. Our task is considerably complicated by the fact that there is a substantial disparity between generally accepted and frequently repeated ideas about the legal process on the one hand, and how the process actually works on the other. The generally accepted folklore, derived from revolutionary ideology and the dogmas of legal science, has an important effect on the way people act but does not accurately represent their actions.

According to the folklore, legal scholars do the basic thinking for the legal system. They are constantly improving the state of legal science by discovering and organizing fundamental, objective legal truth on which other elements of the legal process can then build. They publish the results of their work in books and articles called "the doctrine" and teach the basic principles of the doctrine to students in the universities. The doctrine is the basis of the legal system and is thought to represent objectively stated scientific truth. The doctrine is not law in action, and indeed the scholars would regard attention to such matters as diversionary. They do not consider it their function to enact statutes (as distinguished from drafting codes or other systematic legislation) or to decide cases. They fear that if they became involved in these activities, they might lose their objectivity and perspective, and in any event would be misusing their time, which should be spent on more fundamental, and hence more valuable, work. For a slightly different set of reasons, scholars believe it important to avoid focusing on social, economic, political, or other nonlegal matters, or committing themselves to a particular theory of justice. They believe that they should be uncommitted to any ideology or any objective other than truth—a pure scientist, distinct from the legislators and judges, whom they see as, at most, engineers.

The legislators, representing the people and operating in the area of practical politics, have quite different obligations. It is they who must relate economic and social demands to the legislative process, producing laws that respond to people's needs and desires. In enacting such legislation, however, the legislators must never lose sight of the basic truth of the sort provided for them by the legal scientist. They will find this truth not only in the doctrine but also in systematic legislation enacted by earlier legislators with the assistance of scholars, particularly in the basic codes of the jurisdiction. Thus, new legislation should employ the concepts and institutions and follow the organization established by the scholars and embodied in earlier systematic legislation. The primary function of legislation is to supplement the codes where necessary and to perfect prior legislation, including that of the codes, where it is shown by the continuing investigations of legal scientists to be defective. If the legislature follows the instructions of scholars, it will avoid the danger of incompleteness or lack of clarity and produce legislation that is systematic and, according to the criteria of legal science, valid. Legal scientists will criticize legislation, but not on the basis of its probable social or economic effects. They will discuss its consistency with the tenets of legal science, the quality of its draftsmanship, and its compatibility with the established conceptual system.

Judges, according to the folklore, are merely the operators of a machine designed by scientists and built by legislators, and indeed, one commonly finds judges referred to in the literature of the civil law world as "operators of the law." In deciding a case, the judge extracts the relevant facts from the raw problem, characterizes the legal question that these facts present, finds the appropriate legislative provision, and applies it to the problem. Unless the legal scientist and the legislator have failed in their functions, the task of the judge is a simple one; there is only one correct solution, and there is no room for the exercise of judicial discretion. If the judge has difficulty finding the applicable provision or interpreting and applying that provision to the fact situation, then one of the following people must be at fault: the judge, who does not know how to follow clear instructions; the legislator, who failed to draft clearly stated and clearly applicable legislation; or the legal scholar, who has either failed to perceive and correct defects in the legal science or has failed to instruct the legislator and judge properly on how to draft and apply statutes. No other explanation is permissible. If everyone did his or her job right, the judge would have no difficulty in finding, interpreting, and applying the applicable law. Difficult cases are rare and should be treated as pathological examples. Their existence does not impair the general validity of the working model of the legal process. In the pathological case, it is desirable that the legal scientists immediately examine and propose a remedy for consideration by the legislator. There is consequently bound to be a certain amount of doctrinal discussion of problems of interpretation and application of the law so long as the legal order remains imperfect. Pending action by the legislator, of course, judges should be, and actually are, influenced by doctrinal interpretation.

Hovering over the entire legal process is a brooding anxiety about certainty. The legal scholar seeks to make the law more certain by making it systematic. Certainty requires that the law be completely, coherently, and clearly stated by the legislature, and only by the legislature. Judges are restricted to interpretation and application of "the law" in the interest of certainty, and prior judicial decisions are not "law." Judges are also denied the power to temper the rigor of a rule in a hard case. All nonlegal considerations must be excluded from the law in the interest of certainty. Considerations of justice or other ends of the law must be excluded for the same reason. Hard cases, unjust decisions, unrealistic decisions, are regrettable, but they are the price one has to pay for certainty.

This, though expressed in a somewhat exaggerated manner, is the folklore of the working legal process in the civil law tradition. Although many participants in such a legal process believe in and strive to act according to this model, there are several ways in which practice differs from theory. First, legal science does not speak with one voice. It is common for different schools of thought to be at war with each other over matters that are fundamental to the legal structure, as well as over the merits and defects of specific pieces of legislation or specific judicial decisions. In fact, at any given moment one can find within the scholarly community of the civil law world many different points of view about most legal problems. Even within the relatively monolithic tradition of pure legal science, a little investigation reveals that basic propositions supposed to be objective actually conceal fairly important value judgments. Jurists of the left have tirelessly and shrilly complained of the ideological bias of European legal science for more than a century. They see much of the supposedly disinterested legal scholarship that emerged in the civil law world in the nineteenth and twentieth centuries as a kind of apologia for the institutions and values of nineteenth-century bourgeois liberalism.

Although the legislature tries to provide a clear, systematic legislative response for every problem that may arise, legislative practice falls far short of this objective. As a result, judges have a lot of interpreting to do. They frequently find themselves confronted by problems in which the only applicable legislation is so general as to be useless, is unclear or contradictory in application, or is obviously the product of a legislature that did not foresee the problem now facing the judge. Because in all jurisdictions judges are required to decide the cases before them and cannot give up on the ground that the law is unclear, judges continually make law in civil law jurisdictions. Given inadequate legislative direction, on the one hand, and the command to decide the case, in any event, on the other, they improvise. The judges may try to show how their decisions proceed logically from the rules stated by the legislature. Even when judges believe this to be the case, however, they are still making law. In nations with old codes, the cumulative effect of this kind of judicial lawmaking is particularly obvious. In France, for example, where the Code Napoléon is still in force, the law of torts is almost entirely the product of judicial decisions based on a few very general provisions of the code.

The effect of this kind of lawmaking is compounded by the fact that decisions of the high courts, and some decisions of lower courts, are regularly published (although often in truncated form, frequently lacking the full statement of the facts we are used to in our own judicial opinions), and are cited before courts in subsequent cases. The way of lawyers with difficult legal problems is made much easier if they can find reported judicial decisions interpreting the statutes in question. The same, of course, is true for judges. It is true that they are, at least in theory, free to ignore the prior decision if they think it wrong. But in fact, if the prior decision is by a court above theirs in the judicial hierarchy, they will probably follow it even if they doubt its correctness, because they do not wish their ruling to be reversed. Where the prior decision is one pronounced by the Supreme Court of Cassation or its equivalent, one of whose historical functions has been to provide a final authoritative interpretation of the statutes, the lower judges will probably follow it. The fiction is that they cite and follow the prior decision because it agrees with their own thinking about how the law should be interpreted and applied. The fact is that they follow it for reasons that are inconsistent with the prevailing model of the legal process.

85

The gap between the model of the legal process that has grown out of the civil law tradition, on the one hand, and what people and institutions actually do, on the other, is widely appreciated in the civil law world. Although a great deal of scholarly energy and ingenuity is devoted to proving that the gap is not really there, a growing number of scholars, legislators, and judges have reacted against the traditional model. There has been no revolution in legal thought as drastic as that produced by the legal realism movement in the United States (and, it should be noted, in Scandinavia), but there is a growing tendency to blame the traditional model for failures of justice, popular dissatisfaction with the legal system, and the dragging pace of social and economic development. There is a growing tendency to question the relevance of the traditional, doctrinally oriented system of legal education, and of the products of that system, to the process of decision making in the public and private sectors of national life. The ability of scholars working in the tradition of pure legal science to design a satisfactory law machine is in doubt. The dogma of legislative infallibility has been fundamentally shaken. The image of the judicial function steadily expands. Lawyers in other parts of the world are asking themselves whether ideas about the legal process that emerged from the peculiar conditions of revolutionary France and nineteenth-century Germany are necessarily valid for other nations in other times. The folklore is clearly losing its power, but until some new, acceptable, coherent view of the legal process appears to replace it, it will continue to occupy the field. It is still the residual model of the legal process, and even scholars who recognize that this model is not working spend more effort trying to perfect its basic design than in trying to design a better model.

One reason a new model has not appeared may be the implied threat it poses to continued domination of the legal process by scholars. Although it would be grotesque to suggest the existence of some sort of collusion among scholars, the fact is that the model of the legal process we have been discussing in this chapter was created and has been happily perpetuated by scholars. Attempts in the civil law world to introduce the jurisprudence of interests, legal realism, the law and society approach, law and economics, and law and policy analysis—to mention several coherent attacks on the traditional model—have encountered resistance. They have not been ignored, but they have not penetrated deeply into the legal consciousness. All these approaches would call for more interdisciplinary analysis, for a revaluation of the role of judge in society, for questioning many of the assumptions of the civil law tradition. But the scholars who promote them discover that law schools are difficult fortresses, and traditionally minded lawyers are stubborn and a little deaf. Nevertheless, the civil law tradition is full of innovative people and no definitive battle has been lost. We will revisit this topic in the final two chapters.

XIII

THE DIVISION OF JURISDICTION

THE TYPICAL common law country has a unified court system
that might be represented as a pyramid with a single supreme
court at the apex. Regardless of the number of different kinds of
courts and of the way jurisdiction is divided among them in lower
parts of the pyramid, every case is at least potentially subject to final
scrutiny by one supreme court. The decision in a criminal action, in
a private action between parties to an automobile accident or contract, on a complaint by a citizen concerning the legality of administrative action, on an argument about constitutional rights, and on
appeal from an award of compensation by an administrative tribunal—all may be reviewed by the same high court. It seems entirely
natural to us that the ultimate power to review the legality of
administrative action and the constitutionality of legislative action,
as well as to hear and finally decide the great range of appeals in
civil and criminal disputes, should be lodged in a supreme court.

Matters are typically quite different in the civil law world. There it
is usual to find two or more separate sets of courts, each with its own
jurisdiction, its own hierarchy of tribunals, its own judiciary, and its
own procedure, all existing within the same nation. A case falling in
one jurisdiction will be immune from consideration, whether at the
trial or at the appellate level, in the others. If the typical common
law judicial system can be represented as a pyramid, the typical civil
law judicial system must be visualized as a set of two or more distinct
structures.

The most important of these jurisdictions, the one that impinges
most obviously and frequently on the life of the ordinary citizen,
is the system of so-called ordinary courts. Such courts, staffed by
"ordinary" judges, hear and decide the great range of civil and criminal litigation. They are the modern descendants of the various civil
courts that existed in Europe during the period of the *jus commune*
and that were a major object of revolutionary reform. When one
speaks of civil law judges, one usually means the ordinary judiciary.
The theory of the separation of powers, insofar as it concerns the

judiciary, applies to the ordinary judiciary. It is the ordinary judges whose primary concern is the interpretation and application of the basic codes. When, with the rise of the modern nation-state, the administration of justice was taken out of ecclesiastical, local, and private hands and was nationalized, the ordinary courts became the principal instrument of the state's monopoly on the administration of justice. The legislature was given a monopoly on the nationalized process of lawmaking. The ordinary judiciary was given a monopoly on the nationalized process of adjudication.

The ordinary jurisdiction, as it exists today in France, for example, is really a composite of a number of jurisdictions having separate historical origins. At the core is the sort of adjudication performed during the period of the *jus commune* by local courts in the common run of secular civil and criminal disputes. Later, as the civil jurisdiction of the ecclesiastical tribunals gradually diminished and finally disappeared, the power formerly exercised by them was absorbed by the civil courts. The commercial courts, originally established by merchants to adjudicate their disputes, eventually were nationalized and incorporated into the judicial system. In France and a few other nations, commercial courts still maintain a separate identity at the trial level, but they are subject to the same appellate jurisdiction as ordinary trial courts. In others, such as Italy, the evolution has gone a step further; commercial jurisdiction has become part of the ordinary jurisdiction at every level, and separate commercial courts no longer exist.

At the apex of the system of ordinary courts in France, and in those nations that have followed the French model, is the Supreme Court of Cassation, a body that, as we have seen, originated as a nonjudicial tribunal, created to provide authoritative answers to questions of interpretation of statutes referred to it by the ordinary judges. Even though this nonjudicial tribunal has become the highest court in the ordinary judiciary, its actual jurisdiction still shows the signs of its origins. In Italy, for example, the Supreme Court of Cassation hears only questions of "interpretation and application of the law." Hence, a party to an action can have a hearing before the Court of Cassation only if he or she can phrase his or her objection so as to call into question the way the lower court interpreted or applied a statute, a regulation, or custom. An argument that the lower court misconstrued or misapplied a contract, a will, or a corporate charter is not a question of interpretation of "the law" (although often it can

89

easily be converted into one), and hence cannot be made before the Court of Cassation. Arguments about the facts of the case are also excluded; the only permissible questions are questions of law.

Further, the Court of Cassation decides only the question of law that has been referred to it; it does not decide the case. If it finds that the lower court's interpretation was correct, it says so. If it finds that the lower court made an error in interpretation, it explains what the correct interpretation is, quashes the decision, and orders the lower court (or another court at the same level) to reconsider the case.

The ordinary jurisdiction in a typical civil law nation thus combines elements of jurisdiction formerly distributed among the civil courts of the period of the *jus commune*, the ecclesiastical courts, the commercial courts, and the special tribunal created after the French Revolution to deal with problems of interpretation of statutes. In civil (i.e., noncriminal) matters the ordinary courts apply the law found in the civil and commercial codes and in the legislation that supplements them. Their procedure in such cases is governed by the code of civil procedure. In criminal cases the courts apply the law found in the penal code and legislation supplementary to it; their procedure in such cases is governed by the code of criminal procedure. The ordinary courts also regularly apply a great deal of law that is not contained in these five basic codes and their supplementary legislation, but it is still the tendency to regard the ordinary jurisdiction and the basic codes as functionally equivalent to each other.

A typical civil law nation will also have a set of administrative courts, entirely separate and exercising an independent jurisdiction. The basic reason is, again, the revolutionary doctrine of separation of powers. One of the complaints against the judiciary (i.e., the ordinary judiciary) in prerevolutionary France was that the judges wrongly interfered with the administrative work of the government in a variety of ways. In England the courts had the powers of mandamus (to compel an official to perform a duty) and quo warranto (to question the legality of an act performed by a public official). In France, by contrast, one objective of the revolutionary reforms was to deprive ordinary judges of any power to determine the legality of administrative action or to control the conduct of government officials. Just as the separation of the legislative and judicial powers denied judges any opportunity to interfere in the legislative process, so the separation of the administrative and judicial powers denied them that opportunity in the administrative process.

The notion that the legislature was to be the supreme source of law meant that there could be no inherent administrative power. The administration was to function only to the extent and within the limits of the authority granted it by the lawmaker. Accordingly, every administrative act was potentially subject to the test of legality, and some body other than the judiciary—which was excluded by the doctrine of separation of powers—was needed to rule on the legality of administrative action. In France this need was met by the Council of State, which began as a body of advisers to the king and gradually became the central organ of governmental administration. To its administrative functions was added that of hearing and deciding complaints concerning the legality of administrative action, and the section of the Council of State that regularly exercised this power soon developed judicial characteristics. It has its own procedure and its own catalogue of remedies, and it has built, on a slender statutory base, an immense body of case law that is regularly published and used by lawyers. The landmark decisions (*les grands arrêts*) of the Council of State are a principal source of French administrative law. A number of other nations, including Belgium and Italy, have followed the French model and allocated similar administrative jurisdiction to their own councils of state. In other nations, like Germany and Austria, administrative courts, as such, have been created.

The theory is that the ordinary and administrative jurisdictions are separate and exclusive, so that a case falls into one or the other, but never both. Occasionally, however, a doubtful case arises; if such a case is brought before the administrative court, for example, the defendant argues that it properly belongs in the ordinary jurisdiction. Despite the best efforts of scholars and legislators, no simple, infallible test has yet been devised, and accordingly the matter is settled by litigation. Three examples of the procedure for deciding this question in Europe are instructive. In Italy, the Supreme Court of Cassation is the ultimate authority on conflicts of jurisdiction between the ordinary and the administrative courts. In France the question is finally settled by a special court, called the Conflicts Tribunal. In Germany the court in which the action is brought decides whether or not it has jurisdiction. Its decision can be appealed within its jurisdiction, but it is not subject to further review.

When, after World War II, it was decided to establish rigid constitutions in Germany and Italy, some method of reviewing legislative action for constitutionality had to be found. It was desirable that decisions of unconstitutionality be binding on other agencies of government and also in subsequent cases (i.e., that they have *erga omnes* effects). It was clear that this power could not be exercised by the judiciary (i.e., the ordinary judiciary) without violating the doctrine of separation of powers and limiting the supremacy of the legislature. The kind of thinking that had led to the creation of a separate jurisdiction to review the legality of administrative action led the Germans and Italians to establish separate constitutional courts for this purpose. Although civil law fundamentalists have occasionally argued that these tribunals cannot really be courts or the officials who lead them judges (because courts and judges, properly speaking, merely interpret and apply the law made by the legislature), this view has yielded to the kind of relaxation of principle that led people to regard the Council of State as a court and the officials who run it as judges. The principle of separation of powers and the traditional civil law image of the judicial function continue to apply to the work of the ordinary judiciary. Separate administrative and constitutional courts are not thought to violate that principle.

Consequently, it is common throughout the civil law world to find separate sets of courts performing the functions that fall within unified systems in the United States and other common law nations. In some nations in Latin America, however, where the influence of the American Revolution and the constitutional law of the United States were particularly strong at the time of independence, unified judicial systems were established. The pattern varies from one nation to another. Where a unified judicial system exists, it reflects a more general phenomenon: the substantial influence of the North American model on Latin American constitutional law, as compared to the minimal North American influence on Latin American private law. For reasons that are explained in a later chapter, however, the supreme courts in such unified jurisdictions either have never attained the prestige or exercised the power of the North American model or have only recently attained it.

XIV

LEGAL CATEGORIES

IT IS obvious enough that the law can be divided in various ways
to serve a variety of functions. It is equally obvious, though more
difficult to demonstrate, that any division of the law is bound to
shape the legal system. The conventional way of dividing the law
becomes a part of the law itself, affecting the way that law is formulated and applied. Thus, the manner in which the law is divided and
classified will affect such activities as characterization (how shall
a problem be characterized for legal treatment), teaching (which
courses will make up the law school curriculum), scholarship (what
are the typical fields of specialization among legal scholars), organization of law libraries (how shall books be classified), codification
(what constitutes an appropriate area of the law for codification),
legal writing and publishing (what will be the area of concern of
a book or a legal periodical), and ordinary communication among
lawyers. The generally accepted way of dividing and classifying the
law in the civil law world is quite different from that to which the
common lawyer has been accustomed.

One of the most characteristic aspects of the traditional civil law
way of dividing law is the measurably greater degree of emphasis on,
and confidence in, the validity and utility of formal definitions and
distinctions. While common lawyers tend to think of the division
of the law as conventional—that is, as the product of some mixture
of history, convenience, and habit—the influence of scholars and
particularly of legal science has led civil lawyers to treat the matter of division of the law in more normative terms. As we saw in
Chapter X, definitions and categories are thought to be scientifically
derivable from objective legal reality. Once scientifically found and
refined, they are incorporated into the systematic reconstruction of
the law that is the subject matter of legal science. Thus, the descriptive merges into the prescriptive. The emphasis of legal scholars
on system, abstraction, formalism, and purity further amplifies the
apparently authoritative impact of the distinctions and definitions
of legal science. The definitions and categories become part of the

93

systematic legal structure that is employed by legal scholars, is taught to law students, and is thereby built into the law. Their methodological utility is considered incidental to their essential validity.

The main division of law in the civil law tradition is into public law and private law. This distinction seems to most civil lawyers to be fundamental, necessary, and, on the whole, evident. Treatises, monographs, and student manuals all contain discussions of the dichotomy, often in confidently dogmatic terms that put to rest incipient doubts. European or Latin American law students, who encounter this sweeping division at the outset of their careers, tend uncritically to absorb it. It quickly becomes basic to their legal outlook. Some legal scholars attack the dichotomy (which the English jurist T. E. Holland termed "the mighty cleavage") as being neither fundamental nor necessary, and certainly not clear; but such doubts seldom occur to average civil lawyers. They *know* that public law and private law are essentially different. Where classification as one or the other seems difficult, they are encouraged to blame the positive legal order for not yet adequately comprehending and articulating the true nature of the underlying reality. Fortunately, legal scholars continue to work on such problems, and eventually, they believe, legal science will make it all clear. Meanwhile, statutes, decisions, and doctrine that either assume or attempt to clarify the dichotomy continue to appear, embedding it ever deeper in the law. Examining the origins and the current "crisis" of the distinction is an interesting way to learn more about the civil law tradition.

The distinction between public law and private law has a long history in the civil law tradition. There is some uncertainty about whether it first appeared in classical Roman law or only later, in the *Corpus Juris Civilis* of Justinian, but there is no doubt that the glossators and commentators made the distinction in their writing and teaching. It became a part of the common store of assumptions of the *jus commune*, and it was actively employed during the process of codification and reform in the nineteenth century. When, later in the same century, the law was subjected to the scrutiny of legal scientists, the division between public and private law became basic to their systematic reconstruction of the legal order. The continuous history of the cleavage gave it authority and built it into the culture. Concepts that had been used by legal scholars for many centuries seemed fundamental, necessary, and evident.

Much of the force behind the public law–private law cleavage in modern European legal thought is ideological, the expression of those currents of economic, social, and political thought dominant in the seventeenth and eighteenth centuries that found expression in the civil codes of France, Austria, Italy, and Germany in the nineteenth century. This codified civil law was the heart of private law, and the dominant concepts of the codes were individual private property and individual freedom of contract. This individualistic emphasis was an expression in forensic terms of the rationalism and secular natural law of the age. The emphasis on rights of property and contract in the codes guaranteed individual rights against intrusion by the state. The civil codes were thought of as serving something like a constitutional function. Private law was that area of the law in which the sole function of government was the recognition and enforcement of private rights.

Accompanying this basic attitude were various corollary assumptions. Among these were a rather primitive view of the economy, in which the principal actors were private individuals, and an extremely limited view of the appropriate sphere of government activity. Neither associations of individuals engaged in concerted activity, such as corporations and labor unions, nor broad participation by government in the economic and social life of the nation—both familiar to us in the twenty-first century—was contemplated. The only actors in the legal universe were the private individual and the state, and each had its domain: private law for one and public law for the other.

In the legal scholarship of the nineteenth century this ideology was accepted, at times perhaps without question. Indeed, much of the effort of legal science went into the construction of theories that embodied, but did not directly express, the essentials of what is commonly called nineteenth-century liberalism. One of the major achievements of the German Pandectists was to raise this ideology to a highly systematic and abstract level in the name of legal science; they did it so well that these essentially nineteenth-century attitudes have been preserved in much of the European and Latin American legal scholarship of the twentieth century. The fundamental concepts of the German doctrine are juridical formulations of the role of individual autonomy in the law, and they operate in an area coterminous with that of private law.

It was a kind of negative implication of this private law ideology that an entirely different attitude was appropriate in public law matters.

There the role of government was not limited to the protection of private rights; on the contrary, the driving consideration was the effectuation of the public interest by state action. Public law had, from this point of view, two major components: constitutional law in the classic sense (the law by which the governmental structure is constituted) and administrative law (the law governing the public administration and its relations with private individuals). In private legal relations, the parties were equals and the state the referee. In public legal relations, the state was a party, and as representative of the public interest (and successor to the prince) it was a party superior to the private individual. The development of these two quite different ideologies of private law and public law further embedded the distinction in the legal order.

It has been shown in Chapter XIII that the existence of two sets of courts—the administrative courts and the ordinary courts—was related to the separation of powers doctrine. There has been a good deal of discussion, legislation, and litigation in civil law countries about the division of jurisdiction between the two. In no country is the distinction between public law and private law entirely congruent with that between administrative and ordinary jurisdiction. (For one thing, criminal law, invariably classified as public law by Europeans, is uniformly kept in the ordinary jurisdiction.) There remains, however, a rough correspondence between private law and ordinary jurisdiction, as in Europe the ordinary courts have traditionally been the ones in which controversies about private rights have been decided. This does not mean that all public law questions (other than criminal matters) are exclusively in the administrative jurisdiction and all private law questions (in addition to criminal matters) are in the ordinary jurisdiction. The matter is much more complicated than that, but the public law–private law distinction is closely related to the phenomenon of the separate system of administrative courts on the Continent and elsewhere in the civil law world.

Thus, a variety of influences combine to give the distinction a special importance in the civil law tradition: (1) scholars, particularly legal scientists, with their emphasis on systematic conceptual structures and their ability to convert the descriptive to the prescriptive; (2) tradition, as the distinction figures importantly for at least fourteen centuries; (3) ideology, deeply embedded in the ostensibly value-free concepts of legal science; and (4) the division of jurisdiction between ordinary courts and administrative courts. Meanwhile, there have been great changes in government and in economic and social institutions, and consequently a substantial disparity between the bases of legal theory and the facts of contemporary life is now apparent. The distinction is in crisis, and this crisis is the subject of a good deal of lively discussion in European juridical circles. It may be useful to examine briefly some of the reasons.

First, civil lawyers have learned a great deal about the common law. It might have been possible for a parochial Continental jurist of the nineteenth century to believe that the common law was crude and barbarous by comparison with the civil law. But increased cultural interaction between the civil and common law worlds, and in particular the flowering of comparative legal studies on the Continent, have revealed to civil lawyers that Anglo-American common law is not measurably less sensitive, efficient, or just than their own legal system. They are aware that other Western, democratic, capitalist societies than their own have been able to reach an advanced state of legal development without making a technical distinction between public law and private law. This need not lead them to conclude that their own legal system should discard the dichotomy, but it does suggest that it is not a necessary part of every developed legal order.

Second, the Nazi regime in Germany, the Fascist period in Italy, the socialist legality in the Soviet Empire, and a variety of totalitarian governments in Latin America in the twentieth century tended to dispel the comfortable illusion that the traditional civil law conceptions of public law and private law expressed ideologically neutral scientific truth. As civil law in Europe became ideologically heterogeneous, familiar legal terms took on unfamiliar meanings. The contrasting assertions of social reformers that "all law is public law" and of Lenin that "all bourgeois law is private law" illustrate the point. Astute civil lawyers have always been aware that these conceptions had, at bottom, an ideological basis, but the political history of the twentieth century broadened and intensified that awareness. Such terms as public law and private law do not import any given meaning; their meaning is supplied by the culture of a given time and place. Both those who attack and those who defend traditional conceptions have underlined this truism. Moreover, the twentieth-century events showed that the distinction between private law and public law could not guarantee a sphere of individual freedom where the state could not intervene.

Third, governments have changed; today it is common for the state to become involved in the society and the economy. The individualistic state of the nineteenth century was replaced by the social state of the twentieth. The expanded role of government has often been viewed as leading to a contraction of the area set off for private autonomy. According to one view, fundamental private law concepts have consequently been modified by the addition of social or public elements; such terms as the "socialization" or "publicization" of private law are frequently encountered in the literature. Modern constitutions, starting with the Mexican Constitution of 1917 and the Weimar Constitution of 1919, explicitly limited private rights in the public interest, producing what civil lawyers commonly refer to as the "social function" of property and other private rights. Although a more traditional doctrinal writer may insist that the legal, as distinguished from the social and economic, content of private rights remains unchanged under the new governments, such a distinction is unconvincing. Enormous business conglomerates in areas such as banking, electricity production and distribution, telecommunications, transports, and media, are "private" persons that perform public function. They usually are heavily regulated and controlled by administrative bodies. In fact, the content of private rights has been substantially altered.

Fourth, the involvement of the state in the economic life of the nation has, to a growing extent, been carried on by the direct participation of state entities or state-controlled corporations engaged in commercial or industrial enterprise and using the legal forms of private law. In this way, the private law exerts a growing force on public activity carried on not through the traditional medium of the administration but through the conduct of industrial and commercial enterprise by state organs or by companies controlled by the state. This has been summed up by some administrative law scholars as tending toward a "privatization" of public law, an expansion of the role of private law at the expense of administrative law. The constitutional and administrative law have also changed in emphasis. Administrative law was in great measure the study of the state's privileges and its limitations; the constitutional law, the structure of the state. The primacy of the constitution, the diffusion of constitutional courts, and more recently of human rights courts, have put the focus on the people's *rights* and the obligation of the state's organs to respect rules and rights. The state and the administrative law is not any more what it was in the past.

Fifth, the twentieth century saw the growth in importance and legal recognition of so-called intermediate groups—associations of persons engaged in concerted activity. The earlier image of a legal universe populated solely by the individual and the state, each with its own clearly defined role, is clearly inadequate. In its place is a much more complicated universe, peopled not only by the individual and the state but also by a wide variety of organizations such as trade unions, cooperatives, foundations, commercial and industrial companies, consortiums, and religious societies. Many of these—one need only mention political parties, trade unions, and commercial and industrial corporations—exercise great economic and social power, particularly in postwar democratic societies. They constitute a kind of "private" government, which frequently has greater impact on the lives of large numbers of individuals than do formally constituted "public" governments. In so complicated a legal universe, simple dichotomies like public law and private law seem to lose their utility.

Sixth, European and Latin American constitutions have come to be the medium for the statement of fundamental individual rights, including property rights, guarantees of the right to engage in economic activity, and the like. Thus, the civil codes have been deprived of their constitutional function. That function has been transferred from the most private of private law to the most public of public law sources. In a sense, this might be described as a "constitutionalization" or "publicization" of private law. This development tends to reduce the significance of the public law–private law distinction in the eyes of those who see the distinction primarily as a means of protecting individual rights.

Seventh, rigid constitutions and judicial review of the constitutionality of legislation have been established in most countries of Europe and Latin America. Special constitutional courts exist in some countries, but in others the ordinary judiciary performs this function. This necessarily reduces the significance of rigorous theories about the separation of powers and tends to blur the public law–private law distinction in the minds of those who see a close relation between that distinction and the separation of powers.

Eighth, the substantive differences between public law and private law have been reduced by the action of two separate but related forces. For one, the growth of administrative law has produced progressively greater restrictions on the power of the state to disregard or violate the claims of private persons. Pursuit of the *Rechtstaat*—insistence on the applicability of the rule of law to the state itself—leads ultimately to a homogeneous legal system in which the state is merely one kind, though still a very important kind, of subject of the law. This trend has been reinforced by the efforts of scholars to apply the conceptual structure of traditional legal science, originally developed out of the private law, to public law fields. Together the two trends have produced a strong movement toward "privatization" of public law.

Ninth, the traditional aims and methods of legal science and the general theory of law as taught in the law schools, both largely derived from the work of the Pandectists in the nineteenth century, came under attack during the twentieth century by a small but growing scholarly avant-garde. Others, who view the traditional legal science as valid but spent, seek new directions for the fundamental work of legal scholarship. One result is that the scholars' field of interest has expanded beyond the law itself. They are now concerned about how the law relates to the cultural context from which it draws life and to the society whose problems it must seek to resolve. Another result is a relaxation of emphasis on the validity and usefulness of conceptual structures and logical-formal thinking. The tendency clearly is toward a more "open" jurisprudence and a less technical methodology. In the course of this development, a primarily methodological emphasis on the public law–private law distinction inevitably loses some of its force.

Finally, civil law nations have seen the growth of fields that defy classification as either public or private law. For example, labor law and agrarian law are a mixture of public and private elements, and are incompatible with the traditional classification. Professorial chairs, courses, and institutes in these fields exist in the universities, and journals devoted to them are regularly published. Their existence tends further to blur the distinction between public and private law.

One can say, then, that a rather drastic reshaping of the traditional conceptions of private and public law is under way in the civil law world. The distinction continues, for the reasons mentioned earlier, to have great practical importance. Even under the impact of the forces tending toward newer definitions, substantial areas remain clear, and the great majority of problems and interests remain easily classifiable into one category or the other. But at the frontier between them there is great flux, and few sophisticated civil lawyers today would attempt any functional definition of private law or public law.

The prescriptive effect of the distinction between public and private law tends to overshadow its descriptive utility, but the distinction does also serve a descriptive function. It serves to sum up a division of labor, a separation of the law into smaller parts to facilitate teaching, scholarship, and discussion. But the prescriptive overtones tend to make the distinction a fairly emphatic one, even when used in a descriptive sense. Teachers of private law do not, as a rule, attempt to teach or study the public aspects of their subject. Although they teach about property, for example, they will not discuss property taxation, regulation of urban land use, or the constitutional protection of property rights. These are all parts of public law and are left to specialists in that area.

They also tend to make very sharp distinctions, even within private and public law, between procedure and substance and between one substantive field and another. On the whole, such distinctions seem to be considerably more emphatic in the civil law world than in the common law world. It is unusual for scholars to follow a problem where it leads them, regardless of boundaries, and the notion that one should keep within one's own territory has gradually become an important assumption of the doctrine, and hence part of the law itself. Indeed, in extreme cases, distinctions of this sort are conceived of as embodying reality, as indicating a classification that is not merely conventional but is based on the nature of the material itself. Hence one occasionally finds doctrinal discussion about the autonomy of certain subjects, even where the field under discussion would seem to have been the result more of historical accident than of any inherent qualities. In an aggravated case a writer may insist that only one of various proposed arrangements of the law is correct.

The civil lawyer thus divides the law into public and private law and a group of hybrids (e.g., labor law and agrarian law) that have elements of both. Public law itself is further divided into constitutional law, administrative law, and criminal law. Criminal procedure is generally similarly classified, in part because of its close relation to criminal law. The proper classification of civil procedure has been the subject of considerable scholarly discussion. At present, the dominant view favors considering it as part of public law.

Private law is composed of civil law and commercial law. Of these, civil law is much the more important. It is the modern manifestation of the oldest component of the civil law tradition: Roman civil law. Until the general decline of the temporal jurisdiction of ecclesiastical tribunals set in, the civil law lived in a state of symbiosis with the canon law. When systems of justice were secularized, the civil law survived, greatly enriched by canon law, and the latter lost most of its temporal significance. Today there is a comparable trend toward the absorption of commercial law by civil law.

Commercial law, recall from Chapter I, began as a separate system of justice created by merchants to govern their own affairs. It had its own rules and customs, its own system of tribunals and judges, its own procedures for adjudication and enforcement, and its own constituency. It was not a part of the official systems of civil, criminal, or ecclesiastical justice. These independent features of commercial law have gradually been lost. Commercial justice was nationalized with the rise of the nation-state. The law of civil procedure was extended to proceedings in commercial courts. Gradually the notion of a separate commercial jurisdiction began to disappear. Today, in some nations, separate commercial courts no longer exist, even in name. In others, they have a nominal separate existence at the trial level but are distinguishable from ordinary civil courts only by the presence of a merchant who sits on the bench together with the civil judges. At the appellate level, no distinction exists: the same court that decides civil appeals hears and decides commercial appeals. The commercial court in such a system is no longer a separate court; it is a special subjurisdiction of the civil court.

The commercial law continues to be the object of a separate commercial code in most civil law nations. This, however, is also passing. Both Switzerland and Italy have abolished their separate commercial codes and have combined the matters previously included in them with their civil codes.

Separate chairs in commercial law continue to exist in the universities, and the law libraries of the civil law world contain a substantial literature on commercial law. More and more, however, the trend is toward dominance by the civil lawyers. They are the ones who do the basic theoretical work for the whole of private law (and much of public law). Commercial law doctrine accepts the work of the civil law jurists and builds on it. By a gradual but apparently inexorable process, commercial law has become less a parallel field within the private law area and more a division of, or specialization within, civil law. In addition, a new category called "business law" has developed within private law, fed by both commercial and civil law as well as by tax and labor law contents. Civil law is becoming synonymous with private law; commercial law is being "civilized."

As civil law takes over, and as commercial law gradually loses its separate identity, a process analogous to the enrichment of civil law by canon law is taking place. As a general proposition, the civil law has traditionally viewed transactions between individuals as isolated juridical events. The commercial law, by way of contrast, has viewed transactions involving merchants as a part of the normal flow of commercial activity. The difference in attitude has, through the centuries, produced differences in rules and practices. Not surprisingly, the tendency in modern industrial-commercial nations has been to favor the commercial law approach over that of the civil law. This process, predictably, has been described as the "commercialization" of private law.

Private law thus consists of two major fields existing in symbiosis with each other. Civil law is enriched by "commercialization"; commercial law is diminished by "civilization" and is in decline. The tendency is toward a unified private law that is synonymous with civil law. The oldest subtradition in the civil law tradition lives on, but it is increasingly questioned. There is an abundant bibliography on the publicization of private law, the privatization of public law, the *pénalization de la République*, the constitutionalization of the procedure, and so on. Categories thought to have an ontological character are questioned and their utility placed in doubt. These categories are nevertheless important for the division of university work: there are institutes of private law and public law, or chairs of constitutional law, administrative law, penal law, commercial law, and so on. To the extent that legal scholarship is less centered today on the analysis of legal texts and the construction of concepts, and more interested in the analysis of the role of law in public policy issues or in relation with social and economic problems, these categories are seen as issues of the past. No one would argue any more about the "autonomy" of the labor law or fiscal law as a field. Recent times have seen more of integration, including the perception that law is part of the social sciences and that concepts from economics, sociology, or anthropology are useful for legal analysis.

We return to the rethinking of categories in the civil law tradition in a later chapter.

XV

THE LEGAL PROFESSIONS

L IKE THE divisions of jurisdiction and of law, described in Chapters XIII and XIV, the division of labor among professional lawyers in the civil law world displays characteristics unfamiliar to the common law world, and particularly to those in the United States. Americans usually think of *the* legal profession, of a single entity. To Americans a lawyer, no matter what kind of legal work he or she happens to be doing at the moment, is still a lawyer. Although many young graduates start out as private attorneys, government lawyers, or members of the legal staff of corporations, and stay in those positions for life, it is common for them to change from one branch of the profession to another. During their lifetime lawyers may do a variety of legal jobs. They may spend a year or so as law clerk to a state or federal judge after graduation from law school. They may spend some time in the office of a district attorney or a city attorney, or in the legal office of a state or federal agency, or they may join a corporate law department. They may then move to private practice. If they have a successful career, they may ultimately secure an appointment as a state or federal judge. Most Americans think it normal for lawyers to move easily from one position to another, and they do not think it necessary for them to have special training for any of these different kinds of work.

Things are different in civil law jurisdictions. There, a choice among a variety of distinct professional careers faces young law graduates. They can embark on a career as a judge, a public prosecutor, a government lawyer, an advocate, or a notary. They must make this decision early and then live with it. Although it is theoretically possible to move from one of these professions to another, such moves are comparatively rare. The initial choice, once made, tends to be final in the majority of cases. The point of entry into any of these careers is almost always at the bottom, and advancement is frequently as much a function of seniority within the given career as it is of merit. Accumulated experience in another legal career does not give one a head start or any formal advantage in the process of advancement.

Consequently, many young lawyers soon find themselves locked into a career from which escape is likely to be too costly to contemplate.

A predictable result is a tendency for the lines that divide one career from another to sharpen. Those involved in one branch of the legal profession come to think of themselves as different from the others. They develop their own expertise, their own career image, their own professional association. Rivalries, jurisdictional problems, and failures of communication between different kinds of lawyers are more likely to occur than they are in the United States, with its single, unified legal profession. England, with its division of the profession into barristers and solicitors, stands a step closer to the civil law model but still is far from exhibiting the degree of compartmentalization and immobility one generally encounters in the civil law world. Bureaucratization, especially evident in the various governmental legal careers, is measurably greater than in the common law world, where easy lateral mobility among the different branches of the legal profession leads to a quite different mode of entry into and advancement within them.

The tendency of the initial choice of legal career to be final and the resulting sharp separation of each branch of the legal profession from the others combine to produce a number of effects considered undesirable by many civil lawyers. Frequently the career decision is made without an adequate basis for choice, before young lawyers have been sufficiently exposed to the range of possible legal careers to decide wisely which is the best for them. And the isolation of those in one career from the others, the tendency to identify with only one set of professional interests and functions, encourages a limiting narrowness of attitude and a Balkanization of the legal professions. These are among the reasons why, in certain nations, law graduates are required to undergo a period of practical training, in which they must participate for designated periods in the work of the judiciary, of government lawyers, and of private practice before they can be admitted to any legal career. This institution is most fully developed in Germany, where law graduates have to spend two years (called the *Referendarzeit*) in such a practical training program following their university legal education.

The judiciary provides an obvious and interesting example of the phenomenon we are describing. On graduation from law school (or following the period of practical training, where required) students who wish to become judges immediately apply for admission to the judiciary; if selected (often on the basis of a competitive examination), they enter at the bottom of the profession. In several nations they will attend a special school for judges, but in most cases they will soon find themselves assigned to the lowest in the hierarchy of courts in a remote part of the country. As the result of some combination of seniority and demonstrated merit, they will gradually rise in the judicial hierarchy to more desirable and prestigious judicial positions, and eventually retire. Normally they will compete for desirable positions only against other members of the judiciary. Although appointment to positions on the highest court—a supreme court of cassation or its equivalent—may in theory be open to distinguished practicing lawyers or professors, such appointments are rare. The highest courts, like the lower courts, are likely to employ exclusively those who have risen within the judicial career service. Typically judges will never have practiced law or have served in any other branch of the legal profession, except possibly during required practical training following graduation from the university. They will tend to restrict their professional and social contacts to other judges. They will see the law solely from the judge's point of view. They will be specialists.

Public prosecutors are also civil servants, and, typically, they have two principal functions. The first is to act as prosecutor in criminal actions, preparing and presenting the state's cases against the accused before a court. In this sense the public prosecutors are like district attorneys in a typical American state. Their second principal function, however, is quite different; they are called on to represent the public interest in judicial proceedings between private individuals. Thus, they may have the power to intervene, even at the trial level, in a variety of actions of the sort ordinarily considered private law matters, involving only the interests of the parties. They may also be required by law to intervene in other matters at the trial level, typically actions involving personal status and family relationships. Finally, in some nations, they may be required to appear and to present their own independent view of the proper interpretation and application of the law in actions before the highest ordinary courts. The theory is that a primary function of such courts is the correct interpretation and application of the law, that parties to cases cannot always be expected to present all the arguments, and that the judges need the assistance of a public prosecutor to assure that an impartial view, in the interest of the law, is presented.

Young university law graduates who wish to become public prosecutors ordinarily take the state examination for this career shortly after they leave the university or complete their practical training; if successful, they enter at the bottom of the service and begin a lifetime career in it. Recently there has been a tendency in civil law jurisdictions toward "judicialization" of the public prosecutor service, the idea being that since prosecutors perform quasi-judicial functions, they ought to have something of the independence and security of tenure that is given to judges. This trend has reached an advanced stage in several nations, most prominently Italy, where the office of public prosecutor has been made a part of the judiciary. However, the career of judge and that of public prosecutor continue even in these nations to be separate careers within the judiciary; although the trend ultimately may be toward a merger of the two functions, this has not yet taken place. In particular, the relationship between public prosecutors and the ministry of justice, which exercises authority over the prosecutors' work, continues to be quite different from the relationship of the judge to that ministry. Judicialization of the office of public prosecutor has, however, tended to encourage mobility between the judicial and prosecutorial professions.

In some civil law jurisdictions there is no general career of government lawyer; individual government offices and agencies have their own legal staffs, but appointment, advancement, salary, working conditions, and benefits may vary widely from one agency to another. The lawyer works for a given agency or office and identifies with it rather than, more generally, with a corps of government lawyers. In other countries, there is an office of government attorneys that provides legal services for all state agencies. Even in the former case, appointment and advancement are bureaucratized and regularized. And in either case the difficulty of lateral movement to another branch of the profession tends to fix government lawyers in their careers. As with the judicial service and the public prosecutor service, students who wish to become government lawyers take the state examination after they complete their legal education and practical training, and enter that service at the bottom. Normally they stay with it for life.

The advocate is the closest thing one finds in the civil law to the attorney-at-law in the United States. Divisions of this profession into subspecialties (e.g., the French *avocat* and *avoue*; the Italian *avvocato* and *procuratore*) have disappeared or are rapidly losing their

107

significance. Advocates meet with and advise clients and represent them in court. They may also become involved in helping clients plan their business and property affairs. They will be a product of a university law school and, typically, of a period of apprenticeship in the office of an experienced lawyer.

Traditionally, advocates normally practiced in law offices in which they were the only senior lawyer, with one or two junior lawyers associated with them. Partnerships for the practice of law were forbidden in some countries. European integration and globalization have changed things, and law firms resembling those in the United States have appeared in major cities in the civil law world. Some of these firms are truly international, with branches in several countries, or are branches of huge American or British firms. But even small firms tend to work with foreign associated law firms. In many capitals of Europe and Latin America law firms in which several languages are spoken and written are quite common.

The adoption of the model of the law firm and the generalization of the corporate law department in big business are expressions of the change in the conception of lawyers' role. In France, for example, house counsels were not recognized as lawyers but were classified as legal advisers (*conseillers juridiques*). New rules have erased such distinctions, and *avocats, avoués,* and *conseillers* are now recognized as members of the same profession. The former restrictions had to do with the image of a "liberal" profession, of lawyers as totally independent people who were free to accept or reject clients and who made their own decisions about how clients' affairs should be handled. They were independent professionals paid by the clients, but theoretically their mission was to help justice to be achieved.

Now lawyers are thought of as professionals who can help the businessperson in planning his or her business and in navigating regulations. Their mission is to prevent conflicts or, in case they arise, solve them in an efficient and convenient way. This could entail going to the courts, but doing so is to be avoided if possible. For this reason, it makes no sense to distinguish *avocats, avoués* and *conseillers,* except in terms of considering them as different functions of the same profession. The corporate law departments and the big law firms are only the external or organizational aspect of a change in lawyers' role: from a kind of priesthood to a kind of business.

Generally, all practicing lawyers must be members of a bar association, which frequently is officially recognized and has the authority to establish rules governing the practice of the profession, including fee schedules. As in the United States and elsewhere, members of the practicing bar are likely to become involved in politics and to move into high public office. Although the matter varies from nation to nation, in many civil law countries the percentage of high public officials who began their careers as practicing lawyers is as high as or higher than the United States.

If the civil law advocate closely resembles our practicing lawyer, any similarity between the civil law notary and the notary public in common law countries is only superficial. The historical origins of the civil law notary and the common law notary public are the same, but the two occupations have developed along very different lines. Our notary public is a person of very slight importance. The civil law notary is a person of considerable importance.

Notaries in the typical civil law country serve three principal functions. First, they draft important legal instruments, such as wills, corporate charters, conveyances of land, and contracts. Although advocates sometimes get involved in drafting instruments, notaries continue to do most of this work in civil law nations. (In spite of the notary's established position in this field, however, there is some tension between advocates and notaries over jurisdictional matters.)

Second, notaries authenticate instruments. An authenticated instrument (called everywhere in the civil law world a "public act") has special evidentiary effects: it conclusively establishes that the instrument itself is genuine and that what it recites accurately represents what the parties said and what the notary saw and heard. Evidence that contradicts statements in a public act is not admissible in an ordinary judicial proceeding. One who wishes to attack the authenticity of a public act must institute a special action for the purpose, and such an action is rarely brought.

Third, notaries act as a kind of public record office. They are required to retain the original of every instrument they prepare and to furnish authenticated copies on request. An authenticated copy usually has the same evidentiary value as the original.

Notaries are usually given quasi monopolies. A typical civil law nation will be divided into notarial districts, and in each district a limited number of notaries will have exclusive competence. Unlike advocates, who are free to refuse to serve a client, the notary must serve all comers. This, added to their functions as record office and their monopoly position, tends to make them public as well as private functionaries. Access to the profession of notary is difficult because the number of notarial offices is quite limited. Candidates for notarial positions must ordinarily be graduates of university law schools and must serve an apprenticeship in a notary's office. Typically, aspirants for such positions will take a national examination and, if successful, will be appointed to a vacancy when it occurs, although in some nations the successful aspirant still must purchase the "office" from the owner. Ordinarily there will be a national notaries organization that will serve the same sort of functions for notaries as the national bar association serves for advocates and other organizations for judges, prosecutors, and government lawyers.

We come finally to academic lawyers, who teach in law schools and write the doctrine that, as was explained in Chapter IX, strongly influences all aspects of the legal process in the civil law tradition. They are the inheritors of the tradition of the Roman jurisconsult and of the medieval scholars, whose opinions, at some periods in the history of the civil law tradition, have had formal authority to bind judges. Formal authority aside, academic lawyers are generally viewed as the people who do the fundamental thinking for the entire legal profession. Their ideas, as expressed in books and articles, and their opinions on specific legal questions raised in litigation or lawmaking, particularly in the areas covered by the basic codes, are of substantially greater importance than the work of academic lawyers in the common law world.

It is not easy to become a professor in a civil law university. The road to appointment to a vacant chair is long, arduous, and full of hazards. Young aspirants to an academic career attach themselves to a professor as an assistant, sometimes with pay and sometimes without. Eventually, after meeting certain more or less formal requirements and publishing a book, they will take a state examination for admission to the category of "private docent." If they receive that title, they are considered qualified for an academic post. When a chair becomes vacant, they will compete for it against other private docents and also, if the post is a desirable one, against professors who hold less prestigious chairs. Throughout this process their progress may depend as much on the influence of the professors to whom they have attached themselves as on their demonstrated ability as scholars. This so-called baronial system gives the professor great power over the careers of young scholars. The result is an academic world composed of professors surrounded by retinues of assistants. These assistants are expected to think and work along the same lines as the professor, and thus "schools of thought" are established and grow. Doctrinal, as well as personal, loyalty is expected by the professors, whose power over the assistant's career enables them to demand it.

The uncertainty of success in pursuit of a professorship is so great that few can afford to gamble exclusively on it. In addition, in many civil law nations professors are not expected to spend all, or even a major portion, of their time at the law school. In Latin America, in particular, their rates of compensation reflect this assumption; they are by any standard extremely low. The formal obligations of professors are to lecture to their classes a few hours a week and to give examinations (with the help of their assistants) two or three times a year. They are not paid enough for this to live well, and they consequently divide most of their time between another legal career—usually in practice, in the judiciary, or in public office—and their own and their assistants' doctrinal writing. Although professors are full-time teacher-scholars in some parts of the civil law world, such as Germany, these are exceptions to the general rule. The trend is in the direction of full-time, but it is still only a trend.

In the usual case law professors are also practicing lawyers, the prestige of their title as professor may be of most importance to them because of the business it will bring to their law offices. Advocates with the title of professor will attract important clients and will be called on to prepare opinions on legal questions by other lawyers (and also by judges) and be paid for them.

The tendency of law professors also to be practicing lawyers produces what appears to common lawyers to be a curious sort of professional schizophrenia. As lawyers, they will be pragmatic, concrete, and result oriented. They will follow the problem where it leads them, regardless of boundaries between fields of the law. They will be fact-conscious. They will seek and cite judicial decisions. They will be tough, partisan advocates. As professors, they will write and teach in the prevailing doctrinal style, working in the central tradition of legal science. Both their writing and their teaching will prominently display the academic characteristics typical of legal scholarship in the civil law world, and they may even exaggerate such characteristics to overcompensate because they are also practicing lawyers. They become aggressively academic, as a kind of reaction against their practical work as advocates. Their lives are divided into two separate halves, and they adopt a different professional personality for each.

111

Professors are not all equal. Their prestige differs, and the importance of their opinions is related to this prestige, or *auctoritas*. Usually only the top professors at the most prestigious law schools with a solid number of important publications are accorded the full respect and admiration of their colleagues and other professionals. Traditionally the authors of multivolume treatises commanded the highest *auctoritas*, but in more recent times other criteria have come to command visibility and prestige, such as frequent interviews in mass media within some circles, or international publications and recognition within certain circles.

These, then, are the principal actors in the legal process in the civil law tradition: the judge, the prosecuting attorney, the government lawyer, the advocate, the notary, and the professor-scholar of law. Each is a specialist. The legal profession is a fragmented one, in contrast with the more strongly unified legal profession in common law nations. The difference is an important one; it both reflects and reinforces more fundamental differences between the two legal traditions. These differences can be illustrated by briefly reconsidering the differences between the civil law judge and the common law judge.

We have seen in earlier chapters that civil law judges are relegated to a comparatively minor role in the legal process. According to the common view, their work is, in a sense, routine work. They do not create and formulate policy; they apply rules created and formulated by others, according to procedures they dictate. Consequently, the approach to judicial organization, although it has its own special characteristics, is similar in many ways to the organization of other kinds of civil service. Young people enter at the bottom and advance according to seniority and merit. There are regular procedures for advancement and for periodic evaluations of performance. Because judicial work is viewed as routine and uncreative, it can safely be put into the hands of young, inexperienced people. Such people, it is true, get only minor judicial posts early in their careers, progressing to more important matters as they acquire experience. But it is *judicial* experience that qualifies them to handle the more important work. Experience in other branches of the legal profession does not count.

The prevailing image of the judge tends to become self-justifying. The career is attractive to those with limited ambition who seek security and are unlikely to be successful as practicing lawyers or in the competition for an academic post. Working conditions and rates of pay conform to this image. The better law graduates accordingly looks elsewhere for their careers. There are, of course, some excellent judges, but the best legal minds are usually found elsewhere, particularly in practice and in academic life. The legal profession has a clearly defined class structure; judges are the lower class.

The status of judges thus becomes a fairly reliable index of the continuing strength, within a given nation, of the image of the legal process that grew out of the legal revolution and was strengthened and refined by legal science. Where, as in much of Latin America, the grip of these traditions is very strong, the status of the judiciary is low. This effect is reinforced (and complicated) by the additional factor of social class consciousness. The upper classes, who get the best education and have influential friends, tend to have privileged access to, and to dominate, practice and academic life. Judicial posts are frequently filled by those who are rising to the middle class from humbler social origins.

But where, as in a number of civil law nations, the extremes of the revolutionary model of the legal process have lost much of their power and the grip of legal science on the legal mind is loosening, there is a perceptible tendency toward a judiciary of higher quality and status. It is true that this tendency is strongest outside the ordinary judiciary. The most prominent examples are constitutional courts of the kind originally created in Austria, Germany, Italy, and Spain (described in Chapter XVIII) and later expanded to other jurisdictions and administrative courts like the judicial section of the French Council of State. The international courts, like the European Court of Justice, the European Court of Human Rights, and the Inter-American Court of Human Rights, have also become important legal and political players. But even within the ordinary judiciary, the powers—and hence the status—of the judge have been increasing. The achievement of the French judiciary in creating and developing law in which the Code Napoléon was silent or inadequate is well known. The power of ordinary Italian judges to give a preliminary decision on whether a constitutional objection raised in a civil or criminal proceeding is "manifestly unfounded" is another example. Growing judicial awareness of the close relation between a decision interpreting a statute and the probable result of a constitutional attack on that statute is yet another. Although it is unlikely that replicas of the common law judge will emerge from this evolution, it seems clear that the status of the "judicial class" within the legal profession is growing.

113

XVI

CIVIL PROCEDURE

JUST AS civil law is the heart of the substantive law in the civil law tradition, so civil procedure is the heart of procedural law. Strictly speaking, the law of civil procedure applies only to the process of judicial enforcement of rights and duties arising under the civil law part of private law. The distinct nature and purposes of criminal proceedings and the existence of separate sets of courts, such as administrative courts, have produced separate bodies of criminal procedure and administrative procedure. But all systems of procedure in the civil law tradition have a common origin in Roman, canon, and medieval Italic law. All have tended to follow the lead of civil proceduralists in molding and developing procedural law. Civil procedure is central and basic, and special procedural systems—even criminal procedure—have tended to develop as variations on the civil procedure model.

At the same time, there are important differences between civil and criminal proceedings, and criminal procedure has, particularly since the period of revolutions, been an essentially independent field of regulation and study. Most civil law systems include separate codes of civil procedure and criminal procedure. The subjects are separately taught in the law schools, and a separate literature has grown up around each of them. At a very fundamental level, however, they are based on common notions, and the development of such notions—general theories and general principles of procedure—is traditionally assumed to be the job of the civil proceduralist, just as the development of general theories and principles of law, as shown in preceding chapters, is primarily the task of the civil law specialist.

A typical civil proceeding in a civil law jurisdiction is divided into three separate stages. There is a brief preliminary stage, in which the pleadings are submitted and a hearing judge (usually called the instructing judge) is appointed; an evidence-taking stage, in which the hearing judge takes the evidence and prepares a summary written record; and a decision-making stage, in which the judges who will

114

decide the case consider the record transmitted to them by the hearing judge, receive counsel's briefs, hear their arguments, and render decisions. The reader will observe that the word "trial" is missing from this description. In a very general way it can be said that what common lawyers think of as a trial in civil proceedings does not exist in the civil law world. The reason is that the right to a jury in civil actions, traditional in the common law world, has never taken hold in the civil law world. This tradition continues most strongly in the United States today, where in most jurisdictions there is a constitutional right to a civil jury. (Elsewhere in the common law world the civil jury has been abolished.)

The existence of a jury has profoundly affected the form of civil proceedings in the common law tradition. The necessity to bring together a number of ordinary citizens to hear the testimony of witnesses and observe the evidence, to find the facts, and to apply the facts to the law under instructions from a judge, has pushed the trial into the shape of an event. The lay jury cannot easily be convened, adjourned, and reconvened several times in the course of a single action without causing a great deal of inconvenience and expense. It seems much more natural and efficient for the parties, their counsel, the judge, and the jury to be brought together at a certain time and place in order to perform, once and for all, that part of the civil proceeding that requires their joint participation. Such an event is a trial as we know it.

In the civil law nations, where there is no tradition of civil trial by jury, an entirely different approach has developed. There is no such thing as a trial in our sense; there is no single, concentrated event. The typical civil proceeding in a civil law country is actually a series of isolated meetings of and written communications between counsel and the judge, in which evidence is introduced, testimony is given, procedural motions and rulings are made, and so on. Matters of the sort that would ordinarily be concentrated into a single event in a common law jurisdiction will be spread over a large number of discrete appearances and written acts before the judge who is taking the evidence. Comparative lawyers, in remarking on this phenomenon, speak of the "concentration" of the trial in common law countries and the lack of such concentration in civil law countries. In general it can be said that civil lawyers favor the more concentrated system and that the trend in civil law jurisdictions has been toward greater concentration, with the rate of development varying widely. (Austria and Germany seem to be moving most rapidly in this direction). The tradition, however, continues to be one of relative lack of concentration.

Lack of concentration has some interesting secondary consequences. For one thing, pleading is very general, and the issues are defined as the proceeding goes on; this practice differs considerably from that found in common law jurisdictions, where precise formulation of the issues in pleading and pretrial proceedings is seen as necessary preparation for the concentrated event of the trial. For somewhat similar reasons, the civil law attorney typically spends less time in preparing for an appearance before the court during the evidence-taking part of the civil proceeding. The appearance is usually for the purpose of examining only one witness or of introducing only one or two pieces of material evidence. The pressure to prepare the entire case at the very beginning, felt by the common lawyer preparing for trial, does not exist. The element of surprise is reduced to a minimum, because each appearance is relatively brief and involves a fairly small part of the total case. There will be plenty of time to prepare some sort of response before the next appearance. The lack of concentration also explains the lesser importance of discovery (advance information about the opponent's witnesses and evidence) and pretrial procedures (preliminary discussions with opposing counsel and the judge to reach agreement on matters not really at issue and so on). Discovery is less necessary because there is little, if any, tactical or strategic advantage to be gained from the element of surprise. There is no necessity for pretrial proceedings because there is no trial; in a sense every appearance in the first two stages of a civil law proceeding has both trial and pretrial characteristics.

A second characteristic of the traditional civil law proceeding is that evidence is received and the summary record prepared by someone other than the judge who will decide the case. We have seen in Chapter II that contemporary procedural institutions in the civil law world have been strongly influenced by medieval canonic procedures. In the canon law proceeding, evidence was taken by a clerk, and it was the clerk's written record that the judge used in deciding the case. This procedure eventually was modified to place the evidence-taking part of the proceeding under the guidance of a judge, but quite often the case would still be decided by other judges, or by a panel of judges that included the judge who took the evidence. Comparative lawyers customarily contrast this form of proceeding with the custom in the common law system by which the evidence is heard and seen directly and immediately by the judge and jury who are to decide the case. Accordingly, it has become common to speak of the "immediacy" of the common law trial, as distinguished from the "mediacy" of the civil law proceeding. Here again, comparative commentators tend to think of the common law system as preferable, and there is a steady evolution in civil law jurisdictions toward greater immediacy. The "documentary curtain" that separated the judge from the parties during the medieval period and that was then thought to produce a greater likelihood of fair proceedings, unaffected by influence brought to bear on the judges by interested persons, no longer seems necessary. On the contrary, preparation of the record by someone other than the judge who is to decide the case is now considered a defect because it deprives the judge of the opportunity to see and hear the parties, to observe their demeanor, and to evaluate their statements directly.

In a mediate system, procedure tends to become primarily a written matter. Those in common law countries think of a trial as an event during which witnesses are sworn and orally examined and cross-examined in the presence of the judge and jury. Motions and objections are often made orally by counsel, and the judge rules orally on them. In the civil law, on the contrary, even the questions asked a witness during the civil proceedings are often asked by the judge on the basis of questions submitted in writing by counsel for the parties. Where the practice persists of having one person receive the evidence and make the record and another decide the case, a written rather than oral proceeding is obviously necessary. A trend toward immediacy in civil proceedings carries with it a trend toward orality, and orality is promoted also by the trend toward concentration. Civil law proceduralists think of the three matters as related to one another, and one frequently encounters discussions in which concentration, immediacy, and orality are advanced as interrelated components of proposals for reform in the law of civil procedure.

Foreign observers are sometimes confused by the fact that, in most civil law nations, questions are put to witnesses by the judge rather than by counsel for the parties. This leads some to the conclusion that the civil law judge determines what questions to ask and, unlike the common law judge, in effect determines the scope and extent of the inquiry. People talk about an "inquisitorial" system of proof taking, as contrasted to the "adversary" system of the common law. The

117

characterization is quite misleading. In fact, the prevailing system in both the civil law and the common law world is the "dispositive" system, according to which the determination of which issues to raise, which evidence to introduce, and which arguments to make is left almost entirely to the parties. Judges in both traditions have some power to undertake inquiries on their own, and in Germany the law and the judicial tradition encourage the judge to play an active role in the proceedings. Elsewhere, however, civil law judges are more passive. The common law judge is occasionally inclined to intervene but usually does so only when juveniles or other incapacitated persons are involved in a case, or where there appears to be a clear public interest that the parties are not adequately representing. In similar cases in civil law jurisdictions, a public prosecutor or similar official is required by law to participate in the proceeding as a representative of the public interest. But these are exceptional occurrences, and in the great mass of civil litigation in both traditions the rule is that the parties have considerable power to determine what will take place in the proceedings. Where the civil law judge puts questions to the witness, it is done at the request of counsel, and the questions are limited to those submitted by the lawyers.

The practice of putting the judge between the lawyer and the witness does, however, further illustrate the traditional lack of orality in the civil law. Ordinarily lawyers who wish to put questions to a witness must first prepare a written statement of "articles of proof," which describes the matters on which they wish to question the witness. These articles go to both the judge and the opposing counsel in advance of the hearing at which the witness is to be examined. In this way the opposing counsel (and possibly also the witness) has advance written knowledge of what will go on at the hearing and can prepare for it. This profoundly affects the psychological positions of questioning lawyers and responding witnesses at the hearing, and the fact that any questions the lawyer asks must pass through the judge at the hearing reinforces this effect. The familiar pattern of immediate, oral, rapid examination and cross-examination of witnesses in a common law trial is not present in the civil law proceeding.

Cross-examination, in particular, seems foreign to the civil law proceeding. There has never been a jury to influence. There is little effort to discredit witnesses (in part, perhaps, because parties, their relatives, and interested third persons have been—and in many jurisdictions still are—disqualified from appearing as witnesses). The hearing judge is professionally and impartially interested in getting the relevant facts, and all questions are filtered through the judge. The "offer of proof" determines the scope of the witness's testimony and diminishes the possibility of surprise. Opposing counsel's principal activity in the process often consists only of making suggestions to the judge about the precise wording of the summary of the witness's testimony that goes into the record.

The contrast between common law and civil law procedure, in terms of the interrelated criteria of concentration, immediacy, and orality, can be illustrated by example. The plaintiff's lawyer may propose (in writing) to the hearing judge that a witness be called to testify. A copy of this "offer of proof" will go to the defendant's lawyer. The defendant's lawyer may object, perhaps because he or she believes that the proposed witness is disqualified by a family or business relationship with the plaintiff. The hearing judge will then set a hearing, usually a few weeks later, at which the lawyers will submit written briefs and orally argue the question. The hearing judge will then take the question under consideration and eventually, after a few more weeks, will issue a ruling in writing. If the ruling is in favor of the proposed offer of proof, a date will be set for a further hearing at which the witness's testimony will be taken. In a typical civil action in a common law court, this entire sequence of events—stretching over several weeks or months in a civil law court—would be telescoped into less than a minute of oral colloquy between judge and counsel. Plaintiff's lawyer asks the court to call a witness; defendant's counsel objects and briefly states the reason; plaintiff's counsel replies; the judge rules; and, if allowed, the witness, who is waiting in the courtroom, is called and takes the stand.

Suppose the witness in the previous example is called and testifies. The hearing judge will make notes (there is no verbatim record) of the testimony and dictate a summary to the clerk. After the witness and lawyers agree about the accuracy of the summary, the summary will enter the record that goes to the deciding panel of judges. They in turn must base their findings of fact (and justify those findings in writing) on the record. Even if the deciding panel includes the hearing judge, as it does in Italy, the written record strictly limits the determination of facts. The hearing judge's recollection of the witness's hesitancy, furtive demeanor, or patent insincerity—unless reflected in the written summary of testimony in the record—cannot affect the findings of fact. In the common law, a jury's verdict is

119

summary and requires no specific findings of fact. The witness's demeanor, as well as a variety of other circumstantial factors, can and often will significantly affect the jury's verdict. Where a case is tried in our courts by a judge without a jury, the judge who decides the case is the judge who sees and hears the witnesses. Our procedure permits, indeed requires, judges to base their findings on their observations as well as on the witness's words.

Several factors explain the substantial differences in the law of evidence between the civil law and the common law tradition. One of the most important of these, again, is the matter of the jury. In civil actions in common law jurisdictions, a variety of exclusionary rules, rules determining the admissibility or inadmissibility of offered evidence, have as their prime historical explanation the desire to prevent the jury from being misled by untrustworthy evidence. An alternative policy, one providing that the common law jury be warned of the unreliability of the evidence but then be allowed to evaluate it on the basis of the warning, has uniformly been rejected. The evidence is totally excluded.

The most obvious example is the hearsay rule. Suppose a witness states that he overheard a conversation and is asked what he heard. The immediate response in a trial at common law will be "Objection, your honor, hearsay." The rule is that the witness may not testify about what someone else said. That person should be brought before the court to testify in person, where statements may be subjected to cross-examination, demeanor is observed by the jury, and so on. Accordingly, hearsay testimony is totally excluded. The desirability of such a rule, particularly in nonjury trials, is often questioned, and the rule itself is riddled with exceptions; but it survives to complicate trials and keep otherwise competent and relevant evidence out of common law cases.

Such rules do not exist in civil law jurisdictions because of the absence of a jury in civil actions. This does not mean, however, that evidence can be freely introduced without restriction in civil law proceedings. On the contrary, there are a number of restricting and excluding devices. However, the origin of, and the functions served by, these rules are different from those of exclusionary rules in the common law. To understand these rules we must first go back to the medieval system of "legal proof."

Introduction of the system of legal proof in judicial proceedings was an important civilizing development in European law. It replaced trial by battle and trial by ordeal, the standard methods of deciding litigation in the turbulent feudal world of early medieval Europe. Even though it seems arbitrary, crude, and unjust to us today, this system of legal proof, when it was introduced, exerted a great humanizing influence on the administration of justice and was a long step forward in the attempt to turn judicial proceedings into rational investigations of the truth of conflicting allegations. Civil law judges then, as now, were not very powerful people. However honest they might wish to be, they could not easily withstand persuasion, bribery, or threats—particularly threats made by the wealthy and powerful. To be workable at all, the system of legal proof had to provide some means of protecting judges from such pressures. The means that were developed included a set of formal rules for weighing testimony, a set of exclusionary rules, and the institution of the decisory oath (i.e., an oath that would decide a fact at issue).

The rules governing the weight to be given to certain kinds of testimony were mechanical in operation. The court was required to give predetermined weight to testimony based on the number, status, age, and sex of the witnesses. To prove a fact, a given number of witnesses was required. The testimony of nobles, clerics, and property owners prevailed over that of commoners, laypeople, and those without property. The testimony of an older man prevailed over that of a younger. The testimony of women was either barred or given a fraction of the weight of a man's testimony. These and similar rules for evaluating evidence, in which all evidence was given an a priori arithmetical value (full proof, half proof, quarter proof, and the like), were based on what was believed to be common experience.

The exclusionary rules disqualified certain kinds of people from testifying at all. The principal groups of such people were the parties, relatives of the parties, and interested third persons. Their testimony was considered basically untrustworthy and hence was excluded entirely. This rule protected the parties' conscience against perjury, which they might be tempted to commit to win the case. It may also have reduced the vulnerability of the judge to coercion or bribery.

The decisory oath worked in the following way: Party A could put Party B on his oath as to a fact at issue that was within Party B's knowledge. If Party B refused to swear, the fact was taken as conclusively proved against him. If Party B swore, the fact was taken as conclusively proved in his favor. The compulsion on Party B against swearing falsely lay not only in the religious consequences of a false oath but also in criminal liability for perjury and civil liability for damages.

The early institution of the civil jury in England inhibited the development of some of these restrictions (and led to others) on the introduction and evaluation of evidence in the common law. A group of laypeople was less vulnerable to threats of violence or other forms of influence than was a single judge, particularly if the jurors were the "peers" of the parties, as the common law required. Consequently the need for protection provided to the civil law judge by the system of formal proof was not so strongly felt. The need to protect the jury against unreliable testimony led not only to the disqualification of interested persons as witnesses but also to a set of restrictions on the admissibility of certain kinds of testimony by qualified witnesses. The jury as finder of fact fulfilled the function served by the decisory oath in two ways: it was an effective method of fact-finding, and it relieved the vulnerable judge of the dangers of party influence in deciding the facts. In this way, although the institution of the civil jury developed its own formalistic characteristics, the system of formal proof and the decisory oath failed to develop the importance in the common law that they acquired on the Continent.

Traces of these medieval devices still exist in the civil law world. The mechanical rules of legal proof have evolved into the irrebuttable presumptions of modern civil law. In some civil law jurisdictions, parties are still disqualified from testifying. The decisory oath remains in effect today in many countries (among them France, Italy, and Spain), although its use is primarily tactical. In general, however, the movement for procedural reform has had as its objective what is called "free evaluation of the evidence" by the judge. Such a movement was given great impetus by the rationalist spirit of the revolutionary period, but its thrust has been limited by the general weakness of the civil law judge and by the widespread mistrust of judges among civil lawyers. Nevertheless, proceduralists in civil law jurisdictions generally regard free evaluation of the evidence as the ideal toward which reform should point.

In the United States, if Party A sues someone, he usually must pay his own lawyer, whether he wins or loses. In civil law countries, as in England, the loser usually pays the winner's counsel fees. Although this "loser pays" rule seems fairer at first glance, and may in practice be preferable, it has one significant secondary consequence. To avoid imposing unreasonable counsel fees on the loser, the court uses an official schedule of fees for legal services. The lawyer for the winning party presents an account of services performed, and the court determines the fee that the loser must pay according to the schedule. The lawyer may, of course, have stipulated with the client for a higher fee, but the client is responsible for the excess. It is considered unethical for the lawyer to have a financial interest in the outcome of a case, and contingent fee arrangements are accordingly prohibited in all civil law jurisdictions. The common use of contingent fees in the United States is considered by many civil lawyers to be a shocking practice, although some acknowledge their value as a form of legal aid.

As a general rule there is a right to an appeal in civil law jurisdictions. "Appeal" has a special meaning here that is unfamiliar in the United States, where it is thought of as primarily a method of correcting mistakes of law made by the trial court. In the civil law tradition, the right of appeal includes the right to reconsideration of factual as well as legal issues. Although the tendency commonly is to rely on the trial record as the factual basis for reconsideration of the case, in many jurisdictions the parties have the right to introduce new evidence at the appellate level. The appellate bench is expected to consider all of the evidence itself and to arrive at an independent determination of what the facts are and what their significance is. It is also required to prepare its own fully reasoned opinion, in which it discusses both factual and legal issues.

The use of a jury in civil actions at the common law obviously forestalls review of the factual issues by an appellate court. The jury does not make specific findings of fact; it may, and often does, consider demeanor and other circumstantial factors; it need not justify (i.e., explain) its verdict; and its proceedings are not written. If the appellate court could independently decide factual questions, the jury's role would, in effect, be nullified. As long as there is some factual basis in the record to support the jury's (or the trial judge's) verdict, the appellate court in a common law jurisdiction will honor it.

In addition to the technical appeal, the dissatisfied party typically has the right to a further hearing before a higher court. In some jurisdictions (e.g., France, Italy) this procedure is called recourse in cassation; in others (e.g., Germany) it is called revision. The function, in either case, is similar: to provide an authoritative, final determination of any questions of law involved in the case. Recourse in cassation and revision, in other words, approximates the typical functions of common law appellate courts, which ordinarily restrict

123

their consideration on appeal to questions of law. Recourse in cassation and revision have a somewhat different flavor, however, because of the historical background out of which the courts that employ them have developed.

Recall from the discussion in Chapter VII that the extremes of the revolutionary ideology denied any interpretative function to the courts, and that the Tribunal of Cassation was established in France as a nonjudicial tribunal, to which questions of interpretation of the law would be referred by the courts in order to relieve the legislature of the burden of supplying authoritative legislative interpretations. Over the years, the Tribunal of Cassation has become a recognized court, not only in France but in all jurisdictions following the French model. In these jurisdictions the supreme court of cassation is the highest ordinary court, and it has the function of ensuring the correct observance and uniform interpretation of the law. By a somewhat different but analogous process, the institution of revision was developed in Germany, Austria, and Switzerland. Although there are many important differences between revision and recourse in cassation, these institutions serve similar functions. A high court at the apex of the ordinary judiciary has the power to review decisions of the lower courts to determine whether they have correctly interpreted and applied the law. As in the French case, the Austrian, German, and Swiss courts are also responsible for ensuring the uniform interpretation of the law; consequently, although in theory their decisions are not binding on themselves or on lower courts, theirs is the final voice on the meaning to be given to provisions of law throughout the ordinary courts.

In general, there are no separate concurring or dissenting opinions, even at the appellate level, in civil law jurisdictions. Although exceptions do exist, the general rule is one of unanimity and anonymity. Even dissenting votes are not noted, and it is considered unethical for judges to indicate that they have taken a position at variance with that announced in the decision of the court. A recent tendency toward noting dissents and separate concurrences, and even toward the publication of separate opinions, has developed in the constitutional courts of some civil law jurisdictions. But the standard attitude is that the law is certain and should appear so, and that this certainty would be impaired by noting dissents and by publishing separate opinions.

This rule is evaded in some countries by the occasional practice of a disgruntled judge writing an article for publication in a legal periodical. Even though the article is put in a scholarly or "scientific" form, everyone—lawyers and fellow judges—knows that the article is a way of informing the legal community of the author's dissenting views.

Another fundamental difference between the civil law and common law traditions occurs in enforcement proceedings. Civil law jurisdictions have nothing comparable to the common law notion of civil contempt of court. In Chapter VIII we noted that in the common law a person can be compelled to act or to refrain from acting by the threat of imprisonment or fine for contempt of court—that is, for refusing to obey a court order addressed to him or her as a person. There is, it is commonly said, a wide range of effective action in personam in the common law. The civil law, by way of contrast, knows no civil contempt of court and tends to operate solely in rem. This means that regardless of the type of claim one has against another person, the only way one can collect the claim is by obtaining a money judgment. The reverberations of this difference reach well back into the legal process, affecting, for example, the very legal definition of a contract. According to the civil law tradition, a promise that cannot be converted into money does not create a legal obligation; if the promise is not enforceable in monetary terms (a situation that only rarely occurs), it is not enforceable at all.

The lack of a power to act in personam also affects every aspect of the civil proceeding in the civil law tradition. The power to compel the production of documents, business records, and other evidence or to subject a party or the party's property to inspection is much weaker than it is in common law jurisdictions. Judicial remedies in civil proceedings are restricted almost entirely to remedies that can be enforced against the property of the defendant (e.g., attachment and sale of the defendant's property, delivery of specific property to the claimant, eviction from the property) or acts that can be performed by a third person and charged to the defendant (e.g., destruction of a structure unlawfully built). In the civil law, one who disobeys a lawful order of the court in a civil action may thus be liable to a party for damages (e.g., the French *astreinte*) but cannot be punished by the judge. The most the judge can do is ask that the offender be criminally prosecuted. The only exception seems to be the Latin American *amparo*, an injunction to protect constitutional rights, which gives to the judge a power to arrest in case of disobedience. By contrast, the common law judge in a civil proceeding can punish for contempt.

If one stands back and looks at the two systems of civil procedure, the outlines of two somewhat different ideologies begin to emerge. In the common law world the judge is an authority figure who administers a merged system of law and of equity. (It must be remembered that the court of equity originated as a court of conscience.) Actions are traditionally tried in the presence of a jury composed of a group of neighbors of the plaintiff and defendant who bring to bear throughout the proceeding the prevailing attitudes and values of the community. Employing the civil contempt power, the judge can order people to act or refrain from acting and punish them if they refuse. The whole proceeding is permeated by a moralistic flavor. The parties play out their roles before the parent-judge and the neighbor-jury. In the civil law tradition, by way of contrast, judges are important public servants, but they lack anything like the measure of authority and parental character possessed by the common law judge. Parties and witnesses can disobey orders with less fear of serious reprisal. There is no jury of neighbors to look on, approving or disapproving. The civil law tradition is more thoroughly secularized, less moralistic, and more immune to the ethic of the time and place.

This basic difference in general outlook is dramatically illustrated by the law of damages. In the common law world we see nothing extraordinary in the awarding of penal damages, multiple damages, and so-called general damages (i.e., damages over and above those proved) in civil actions against defendants whose conduct appears to be malicious or grossly negligent. In the civil law tradition, however, such damages are rarely available to a plaintiff in a civil proceeding. The line between the civil and the criminal is more sharply drawn, and morally reprehensible (i.e., malicious or grossly negligent) actions are matters for the criminal law rather than for the civil law. In the civil trial, as a general rule, the plaintiff's recovery is limited to compensation for the loss suffered. If the judgment of the community is going to be brought to bear on a defendant because of the moral character of his or her action, it must be done through the processes of the criminal law, where the defendant is protected from arbitrary or exaggerated imposition of penalties by the principle of the criminal law that no penalty be assessed for something that was not legally defined as a crime at the time the action took place. And, as is generally true of criminal law in Western nations, the penalties in such cases are limited to those established in the statute.

XVII

CRIMINAL PROCEDURE

ALTHOUGH THE revolution profoundly affected every part of the civil law tradition, its effects are most clearly observable in public law. And, within the field of public law, much of the criticism of the ancien régime and much of the call for reform tended to be concentrated in the field of criminal procedure. Among the writers and philosophers of the eighteenth century who contributed to the ideology of revolution, most had something to say about the sorry state of criminal law and criminal procedure. The most important reformer in this field was Cesare Beccaria, whose book *Of Crimes and Punishments* exploded onto the European scene in 1764 and went on to become the most influential work on criminal law and criminal procedure in Western history.

Substantive criminal law in Western capitalist civil law countries does not differ greatly from that of common law countries. The same kinds of actions are considered criminal, and the same general approaches to punishment are discussed and debated throughout Western culture. There are, however, significant operational differences in criminal procedure, and it is striking to observe the extent to which the revolutionary reform of criminal procedure reflects the causes and effects of the revolutionary period in the civil law tradition. We can illustrate this point by examining the principal thesis and the organization of Beccaria's book.

He begins by establishing the principle of *nullum crimen sine lege* and *nulla poena sine lege*. As Beccaria states it: "Only the laws can determine the punishment of crimes; and the authority of making penal laws can reside only with the legislator, who represents the whole society united by the social compact." Thus, according to Beccaria, crimes and punishments can be established only by law, and by "law" he means "statute." Beccaria then proceeds to discuss the interpretation of laws. His position is that "judges in criminal cases have no right to interpret the penal laws, because they are not legislators." And further, "the disorders that may arise from a rigorous observance of the letter of penal laws are not to be compared to

127

those produced by the interpretation of them. . . . When the code of laws is once fixed, it should be observed in the literal sense, and nothing more is left to the judge than to determine whether an action be or be not conformable to the written law." In the same paragraph, speaking of judges, he refers to "the despotism of this multitude of tyrants." Later, in the chapter on obscurity in the law, he says: "If the power of interpreting laws be an evil, obscurity in them must be another, as the former is the consequence of the latter. This evil will be still greater if the laws be written in a language unknown to the people; who, being ignorant of the consequences of their own actions, become necessarily dependent on a few, who are interpreters of the laws, which, instead of being public and general, are thus rendered private and particular." Beccaria goes on to establish two basic principles. The first is that there should be proportion between crimes and punishments, so that more serious crimes are more severely punished. The second is that punishments should apply impartially to criminals, regardless of their social station, position, or wealth.

Observe the similarity of these observations to the general characteristics of the revolutionary legal tradition, described in Chapter III. They are permeated with state positivism, rationalism, and a concern for the rights of man as enunciated by the school of natural law. Principles similar to those stated by Beccaria were, at the same time, affecting the evolution of criminal procedure in the common law world. One difference, however, was the emphasis on, perhaps the exaggeration of, these principles in Europe as a result of the French Revolution and the effect of that revolution on the thinking about law and the state in the civil law world. Hence even today one finds a sharper emphasis in civil law jurisdictions on the principle that every crime and every penalty shall be embodied in a statute enacted by the legislature. To a civil lawyer, common law courts seem to violate this principle every day when they award penal damages, multiple damages, or general damages in civil actions; when they convict people of "common law" crimes; and when they summarily punish people for contempt. Another significant difference between the two traditions is the earlier movement toward reform of penology in the civil law world. Under the influence of Beccaria and his successors, the death penalty was abolished in Tuscany in the eighteenth century, and fundamental reforms leading to less drastic penalties for minor offenses took place throughout Europe well in advance of similar reforms in Great Britain and the United States.

It is obvious that an emphasis on the principle of legality (no crime or penalty without a statute enacted by the legislature), together with a desire to have such statutes written down as part of a rational scheme in a language that could be read by the citizen, should lead to codification of the criminal law. In fact, the first object of codification in revolutionary France was the criminal law, and a criminal code was actually written during the French Revolution. If a case for codification exists, it exists most clearly in the fields of criminal law and procedure. But once the case is made for criminal law, it is easily extended to other fields, particularly in a legal tradition in which judges are distrusted and a representative legislature is a hero. This, as we have seen, was the case throughout the revolutionary period in the civil law world.

One of the most common comparisons one hears made about criminal procedure in the two traditions is that the criminal procedure in the civil law tradition is "inquisitorial," whereas that in the common law tradition is "accusatorial." Although this generalization is inaccurate and misleading as applied to contemporary systems of criminal procedure, it has some validity when put into historical context. In a sense it can be said that the evolution of criminal procedure in the past two centuries in the civil law world has been away from the extremes and abuses of the inquisitorial system, and that the evolution in the common law world during the same period has been away from the abuses and excesses of the accusatorial system. The two systems, in other words, are converging from different directions toward roughly equivalent mixed systems of criminal procedure.

Let us first consider the accusatorial system, which is generally thought by anthropologists to be the first substitute that an evolving society develops for private vengeance. In such a system the power to institute the action resides in the wronged person, who is the accuser. This same right of accusation is soon extended to the accuser's relatives, and as the conception of social solidarity and the need for group protection develops, the right of accusation extends to all members of the group. A presiding officer is selected to hear the evidence, decide, and sentence; this person does not, however, have the power to institute the action or to determine the questions to be raised or the evidence to be introduced and has no inherent investigative powers. These matters are in the hands of the accuser and the accused. The criminal trial is a contest between the accuser and the accused, with the judge as a referee. Typically the proceeding takes place publicly and orally and is not preceded by any official (i.e., judicial or police) investigation or preparation of evidence.

Criminal procedure in medieval civil law also was accusatorial. The *Siete Partidas,* an important legislative compilation of thirteenth-century Castile, describes the criminal procedure as accusatorial; the judges had inquisitorial powers only in cases of lèse-majesté crimes. The inquisitorial procedure developed later in Catholic Church courts in cases charging the crime of heresy. Under the influence of this canonical procedure and the rise of statism in the sixteenth century, all Continental criminal procedure became inquisitorial.

The inquisitorial system typically represents an additional step along the path of social evolution from the system of private vengeance. Its principal features include, first, attenuation or elimination of the figure of the private accuser and appropriation of that role by public officials; and second, the conversion of the judge from an impartial referee into an active inquisitor who is free to seek evidence and to control the nature and objectives of the inquiry. In addition, the relative equality of the parties that is an attribute of the accusatorial system, in which two individuals contest before an impartial arbiter, has been drastically altered. Now the contest is between an individual (the accused) and the state. Historically, inquisitorial proceedings have tended to be secret and written rather than public and oral. The resulting imbalance of power, combined with the secrecy of the written procedure, creates the danger of an oppressive system, in which the rights of the accused can easily be abused. The procedure had a moral purpose: to elicit from the defendant the confession of his crime. As confession was so important, torture was considered legitimate and was regulated. Too harsh a torture will produce false confessions. "Exquisite" (nonregulated) tortures were forbidden.

The most infamous analogue familiar to us in the common law world is the Star Chamber, which was basically an inquisitorial tribunal. The Star Chamber was, however, exceptional in the common law tradition. Historically the system was basically accusatorial in nature, and the early development of the jury as a necessary participant in the criminal proceeding in England tended to prevent any strong movement toward excesses like those of the Continental inquisitorial system. If a jury was to have the power to determine guilt or innocence of the accused, the proceedings would necessarily have to be oral and be conducted in the presence of the jury. Although it became the rule early in the development of the English criminal trial that the accuser need not employ and compensate the prosecuting attorney, the public prosecutor came very late to the common law. Even today, in England, a member of the practicing bar will be retained to represent the public interest in a criminal proceeding and will be compensated from public funds. The creation of a professional police force and of a public prosecutor to investigate the commission of crimes, compile evidence, seek authority to prosecute, and actually conduct the criminal proceeding on behalf of the state is a comparatively recent development in the common law world. In effect, it represents a shift away from the accusatorial and toward the inquisitorial system. But the public nature of the trial, the orality of the proceedings in the trial, the existence of a jury, and the limitations on the power of the judge all combine to perpetuate some of the more desirable features of the accusatory system. The result is a kind of mixed system of criminal procedure.

In the civil law world, the movement toward the extremes of the inquisitorial model was impelled by the revival of Roman law, the influence of canonic procedure, and, most important, the rise of statism. The criminal action was an action by the state against accused individuals. The proceedings were written and secret. The accused had no right to counsel. They could be required to testify under oath, and torture was a common device for compelling testimony and eliciting proof. The judge was not limited to the role of impartial arbiter but played an active part in the proceedings and determined their scope and nature. The prince, as the personification of the state, had the power to punish and to pardon, unrestricted by rules against ex post facto laws, by principles of equal treatment of individuals, or by what we would now call considerations of ordinary humanity and justice.

As a result of the work of Beccaria and others in the eighteenth century, public sentiment against the abuses of criminal procedure became very strong, and reform of criminal procedure became one of the principal objectives of the European revolutions. Reformers of the time pointed to the criminal procedure of England as an example of a just, democratic system, and called for reform of their own criminal procedure along common law lines. Prominent among the demands made were (1) institution of the jury, (2) substitution of the oral public procedure in place of secret written procedure,

(3) establishment of the accused's right to counsel, (4) restriction of the judge's inquisitorial powers, (5) abolition of the requirement that the accused testify under oath, (6) abolition of torture, and (7) abolition of arbitrary intervention by the sovereign in the criminal process, by way of either penalty or pardon.

In the fervor of the French Revolution an attempt was made to abolish the criminal procedure of the old regime wholesale and substitute an entirely new procedure based on the English model. The failure of that effort soon became apparent, and a counterrevolution took place. The result is a mixed system in France, composed in part of elements from prerevolutionary times and in part of reforms imposed after the revolution.

The typical criminal proceeding in the civil law world can be thought of as divided into three basic parts: the investigative phase, the examining phase (the instruction), and the trial. The investigative phase comes under the direction of the public prosecutor, who also participates actively in the examining phase, which is supervised by the examining judge. The examining phase is primarily written and is not public. The examining judge controls the nature and scope of this phase of the proceeding. The examining judge is expected to investigate the matter thoroughly and to prepare a complete written record, so that by the time the examining stage is complete, all relevant evidence is in the record. If the examining judge concludes that a crime was committed and that the accused is the perpetrator, the case then goes to trial. If the judge decides that no crime was committed or that the crime was not committed by the accused, the matter does not go to trial.

In 1975, Germany abolished the examining phase. The entire pretrial process is now in the hands of prosecutors and the police, as it is in the United States. In the trial of important crimes, a panel of judges and laypeople gives the verdict. Trial, which is concentrated, as in the common law, can be avoided by a guilty plea. By the end of the twentieth century several European countries, including Italy, and most Latin American nations had reformed their criminal procedure along the German model. The late twentieth century was a particularly intensive time in reforming the criminal procedure in the civil law world.

In a very general way it can be said that the principal progress toward a more just and humane criminal proceeding in Europe in the past century and a half has come through reforms in the investigative and examining phases of the criminal proceeding. These reforms have been of two principal kinds. First, every effort has been made to develop a core of prosecuting attorneys who should act impartially and objectively. In Italy, for example, prosecuting attorneys are now members of the judiciary, having security of tenure and consequent freedom from influence similar to that enjoyed by judges. Second, a number of procedural safeguards have been developed to help protect the accused's interests during the examining phase. Principal among these is the right of the accused to representation by counsel throughout this phase of the proceeding. This does not mean that counsel for the accused has unrestricted freedom to cross-examine witnesses or to introduce evidence on behalf of his or her client. The examining phase is still conducted by a judge. Counsel for the accused can, however, participate in the proceedings in such a way as to protect the client's interests, calling certain matters to the attention of the court and advising the client on how to respond as the proceeding unfolds. The dossier compiled by the examining magistrate is open to inspection by the defense, routinely providing information about the prosecution's case that in an American proceeding would be unavailable to the defense until its production was compelled by a motion for discovery or it was revealed at trial.

As a rule, defendants can be questioned during the examining phase and at the trial. They cannot, however, be sworn, and they may refuse to answer. Their refusal to answer, as well as their answers, will be taken into account in deciding questions of guilt or in fixing the penalty. Until recent reforms, there was no developed system of cross-examination comparable to the American one, although the prosecutor could suggest questions to be put to the defendant by the judges.

In the American criminal justice system, defendants need not take the stand, and inferences from their failure to testify are prohibited. If they do testify, however, they must be sworn and are subject to cross-examination by the prosecutor. An eminent comparative lawyer has characterized the American system as one that puts the defendant to a "cruel choice" between testifying under oath, subject to cross-examination, and not testifying at all. He suggests that the civil law, by not subjecting the accused to so drastic a choice, is more humane.

As a consequence of the nature of the examining phase of the criminal proceeding, the trial itself is different in character from the common law trial. The evidence has already been taken and the record made, and this record is available to the accused and to counsel, as well as to the prosecution. The function of the trial is to present the case to the trial judge and jury and to allow the prosecutor and the defendant's counsel to argue their cases. It is also, of course, a public event, which by its very publicity tends to limit the possibility of arbitrary governmental action.

In orthodox civil law rhetoric, the guilty plea was admissible as evidence but could not be used to avert the trial. It was for the court to determine guilt, not the defendant or the prosecutor, and plea bargaining accordingly was prohibited. In fact, however, plea bargaining in disguised form was practiced in most, if not all, civil law jurisdictions even while legal scholars denied that it existed and unfavorably compared the civil law orthodoxy to the prevalence of plea-bargaining practice in the United States. It now has been openly accepted in Germany and other major civil law systems as part of the late-twentieth-century reform of criminal procedure described later in this chapter. In Italy, for example, plea bargaining is expressly included in the new code of criminal procedure, which provides for a one-third reduction of the statutory sentence for a defendant who pleads guilty. Plea bargaining is, of course, a way of disposing quickly of the growing number of criminal prosecutions, which far exceed the capacity of the courts in the civil law world, as in the common law world.

One frequently encounters two common misapprehensions about criminal procedure in the civil law world. The first is to the effect that there is no presumption of innocence; the second is that there is no right to a jury trial. As stated, these are demonstrably false. Although the precise nature of the presumption and the degree to which it serves to protect the accused vary within the civil law world, a legal presumption of innocence does exist in most civil law jurisdictions. In those in which it does not exist as a formal rule of law, something very much like it emerges from the examining phase of the criminal proceeding, where the character of the examining judge and judicialization of the function of the prosecuting attorney tend to prevent the trial of persons who are not probably guilty.

The common supposition that there is no right to a jury trial in the civil law world is simply contrary to the facts. The jury or its functional equivalent has been an established institution since the reforms of the revolutionary period. It may not be available for as

134

wide a range of offenses (even in some American states a jury trial is not granted in misdemeanor cases), it may not consist of twelve persons, it may frequently take the form of lay advisers who sit on the bench with the judge, and even where it looks like the American jury, it may not have to render a unanimous verdict of guilty for the accused to be convicted. These are, particularly when they accumulate, important differences between the American conception of a jury and the civil law practices. But the fact remains that the jury is a well-established institution in the criminal proceedings of civil law jurisdictions. France has had the criminal jury since the nineteenth century. The new constitution of Spain, adopted in 1978, provides for trial by jury in criminal cases. Continental lawyers also have an aversion to single-judge courts, summed up in the aphorism *juge unique, juge inique.* Recently the French Constitutional Council held unconstitutional an attempt to establish single-judge courts for cases involving less than major crimes. The usual provision is for three judges at the trial level. Even where there is no jury, the requirement of three judges reduces the danger of an arbitrary decision.

For those readers who wonder which is the more just system, the answer must be that opinion is divided. In 1977 a Harvard professor wrote a book charging American criminal procedure with "denial of justice" and advocating reforms along French lines. Other Americans have sought to prove that their system is fairer to the accused. The debate is clouded by ignorance of the law and practice in civil law nations and by preconceptions that are difficult to dispel. In the end, a statement made by an eminent comparative scholar after long and careful study is instructive: he said that if he were innocent, he would prefer to be tried by a civil law court, but that if he were guilty, he would prefer to be tried by a common law court. This is, in effect, a judgment that criminal proceedings in the civil law world are more likely to distinguish accurately between the guilty and the innocent.

XVIII

CONSTITUTIONAL REVIEW

CONSTITUTIONAL LAW and administrative law make up the basic content of what is called public law in civil law jurisdictions. Constitutional law is the law governing the organization and operation of the state. Administrative law is the law governing the organization and operation of the administrative branch of government and the relations of the administration with the legislature, the judiciary, and the public.

Earlier in this book, particularly in Chapters III and IV, we discussed the nature of the typical centralized state that emerged in Europe in the fifteenth to eighteenth centuries and blossomed in the Western revolutions. This was the modern nation-state—secular, positivist, internally and externally sovereign, a state whose power was exercised through the legislative, executive, and judicial branches of government. Among these, the representative legislature was the supreme power; legislation controlled executive and judicial action. Both legislative and executive action were immune from judicial review or interference.

Much of the development of public law in the civil law world since the revolutionary period can be viewed as a movement away from the extremes of this model. There are many fascinating, interrelated aspects to this movement, of which only two are discussed here: the development of processes for reviewing the legality of administrative action (and hence curbing excessive administrative power) and the trend toward rigid constitutions and review of the constitutionality of legislation.

In Chapter XIII we briefly discussed how the demand for review of the legality of administrative action was met. The widespread distrust of the judiciary, the traditional image of the judge and the judicial function, and the principle of separation of powers made such review by the ordinary judiciary an unacceptable solution. In addition, the insistence that ordinary judges not be lawmakers in any sense led to rejection of the idea that prior judicial decisions should control future judicial action, even with respect to the same administrative act. The absence of such a principle would make judicial review of the legality of administrative action relatively ineffective. A court that was not bound by its own or other courts' prior decisions, and that consequently could make a decision binding only on the parties to the case before it, was inadequate to the task of keeping administrative action within acceptable bounds. What was needed was an acceptable method of deciding *erga omnes*—in a way that would have general effects, not limited to the parties—on the legality of the administrative act in question.

To give such powers to the ordinary courts would thus have required abandonment of a number of basic, deeply felt notions about the proper organization and operation of the state and about the nature and functions of the ordinary courts. As we have already seen, the solution adopted in France, and subsequently in much of the civil law world, was to establish a separate tribunal within the administration. In other nations, including Germany, the same result was achieved by setting up a separate system of administrative courts. Although there are many important differences between the two approaches typified by the French and German solutions, both met the same basic requirements. First, review of the legality of administrative action was kept out of the hands of the ordinary judiciary, and the principle of separation of powers was preserved. Second, a decision that an administrative act was illegal, and therefore void, could be given *erga omnes* effect without introducing the principle of stare decisis into the system of justice administered by the ordinary courts. Although there is great variety in the ways in which individual nations following the civil law tradition have worked out their systems for reviewing administrative legality, the basic pattern described here is the dominant one.

When one moves to the problem of reviewing the constitutionality of legislation, however, matters become more complicated. The difficulties perceived as standing in the way of an effective system of control are generally similar throughout the civil law world, but the movement toward their definitive resolution is not nearly as advanced as that for review of the legality of administrative action. There clearly is movement toward limiting legislative supremacy, but the pace of this movement and the range of solutions adopted vary from one civil law nation to another.

Legislative supremacy and a flexible constitution are companion concepts. If the expressed will of the representative legislature is to have the force of law, and if the legislative act is not subject to judicial or executive control, then it is an easy logical step to the conclusion that an ordinary law can prevail over a conflicting constitutional provision. This does not mean that the constitution loses all force as a basic law establishing a governmental structure and providing rules controlling and limiting governmental acts. Proposed legislation in a nation with a flexible constitution will still ordinarily be adopted within the limits established by current constitutional interpretation, and a proposal to transcend those limits will raise special legislative policy considerations. Where a possible conflict between a constitutional provision and a statute appears to have occurred without conscious legislative consideration, the tendency of the courts will be to interpret the provision and the statute in such a way as to avoid the conflict. In these and other ways, even a flexible constitution has its own special, *constitutional* character.

A flexible constitution, not surprisingly, is quite different from a rigid constitution. Here, however, it is necessary to distinguish between a formally rigid constitution and a functionally rigid one. Formally rigid constitutions, of which there have been a number in the civil law world, specify limitations on legislative power and state special requirements for constitutional amendments, but they make no provision for enforcing these rules. The ordinary courts are, according to the prevailing theory, totally disqualified from interfering in the legislative process. The administrative courts can rule on the validity only of administrative acts, not of legislative acts. In form the legislature is bound by the constitution, but there is no organ of government authorized to decide whether the legislature has exceeded its powers. In a functionally rigid system, such an organ exists and functions.

The original, and still archetypal, example of a functionally rigid constitutional system is that of the United States. The constitutional systems that appeared throughout the civil law world in the eighteenth and nineteenth centuries were sometimes rigid and sometimes flexible. None, however, included functional schemes for reviewing the constitutionality of legislation. The history of constitutional development in the civil law tradition since the revolution has been one of gradual movement toward functionally rigid constitutional systems. For a variety of reasons, however, the methods of reviewing the constitutional validity of legislative action adopted in civil law nations have been quite different from those used in the United States.

The movement toward constitutionalism in the civil law tradition can be seen as a logical reaction against the extremes of a secular, positivistic view of the state. During the period of the *jus commune* and prior to the Reformation, the authority of the Catholic Church and the writings of Roman Catholic natural lawyers about government and the individual provided a set of ideas and values that exerted some degree of restraining influence on the prince and on government officials. Many of these ideas were embedded deeply in the *jus commune* itself. But the authority of the church and of Roman Catholic natural law declined. With the growth of the nation-state the *jus commune* became a subsidiary system, inferior to the national law. At the same time the emphasis in secular natural law thinking on a popularly elected, representative legislature and on the separation of powers, combined with the revolutionary desire to limit the power of judges, produced an exaggerated emphasis on legislative autonomy. The old restraints on government were removed, and in the new positivistic state the representative legislature was given an inflated role and encouraged to be the sole judge of the legality (as opposed to the political acceptability) of its own action. In a sense the trend toward functionally rigid constitutions, with guarantees of individual rights against "unjust" legislative action, can be seen as a process of "codification of natural law" to fill the void left by rejection of Roman Catholic natural law and the *jus commune* on the one hand, and to deflate the bloated image of the legislature that emerged from the revolutionary period on the other.

A desire to review the constitutionality of legislative action does not necessarily lead to the institution of judicial review. On the contrary, fundamental notions about the separation of powers and about the nature and limits of the judicial function in the civil law tradition made constitutional review by the ordinary judiciary an unacceptable alternative. And the rejection of the principle of stare decisis further limited the attractiveness of (ordinary) judicial review. Constitutional questions are of such far-reaching importance that it seemed necessary to have them decided authoritatively, with *erga omnes* effects, rather than accept the hazards of inconsistent decisions by different courts, or even by the same court, in similar cases. But civil law nations could not accept the proposal that the decisions of ordinary courts be given authority as law. Consequently the system familiar to citizens of the United States, in which all courts at every level of jurisdiction have the power to decide constitutional issues with *erga omnes* effects, has generally been rejected in the civil law world. Even where, as in some Latin American nations, some power of judicial review has been given to ordinary courts, the tendency has been to concentrate that power in one supreme court rather than diffuse it throughout the judicial system. This does not eliminate the possibility of conflicting decisions on the constitutionality of legislation, but it does reduce it. The Supreme Tribunal of Venezuela, for example, is the only Venezuelan court with power to review the constitutionality of Venezuelan legislation and declare a statute void. Any other judge who finds a conflict between a legislative rule and a constitutional one will probably apply the constitutional one, but this decision does not void the statute.

A strong movement toward establishment of constitutional review has swept through the civil law world since the end of World War II. The means adopted to achieve it have, however, varied. It is not surprising to find that France, the traditional source of the fundamentalist position on the separation of powers and the role of courts, has a system of nonjudicial review. The government organ that performs this function, established under the 1958 constitution, is called the Constitutional Council (not "Court"). It is composed of all former presidents of France as well as nine additional persons, three of whom are chosen by the president of France, three by the president of the Chamber of Deputies, and three by the president of the Senate. Before promulgation, certain kinds of laws must, and others may, be referred by the executive or the legislature to this council for a decision on their constitutionality. The council must respond within a certain time, after secret deliberations with no contentious procedure, no parties, no oral hearings, and no other marks of judicial proceedings. If the council finds the law in question unconstitutional, the law cannot be promulgated unless the constitution is appropriately amended.

The original composition and procedure of the Constitutional Council made its nonjudicial nature clear. Its function seemed more like an additional step in the legislative process than a judicial proceeding, and it was common to characterize this sort of constitutional review as political rather than judicial. More recently, the work of the Constitutional Council has begun to take on judicial characteristics and to be more frequently perceived, by lawyers and the public alike, as a courtlike institution. Meanwhile, the French Council of State (frequently) and even the Supreme Court of Cassation (very infrequently and narrowly) have become involved in constitutional litigation. Still, the theory remains that there is no judicial review of legislation in France.

The stronger trend in the civil law world today, however, is toward the institution of some form of judicial review. We can best begin to understand this trend by examining another important distinction in constitutional doctrine: that between the formal and the substantive validity of legislation. The question of formal validity goes to whether the legislator has observed the rules set out in the statutes and the constitution to govern the form and procedure of the legislative process—such rules as those governing legislative deliberation, voting, and promulgation. Questions of substantive validity go to the consistency of the substance of the statute with constitutional provisions protecting the rights of the public and of government officials and agencies. (It might be noted that this distinction between formal and substantive validity, though conceptually clear, is difficult to maintain in practice. But that is a topic for another book.)

It is arguable that a formally defective statute is not really a statute, and that it therefore does not qualify as a part of "the law" that judges have the obligation to apply in cases before them. If the legislature has not followed the procedural rules established for the legislative process, according to this reasoning, the product is not legislation and therefore need not be applied by the court. Even in a jurisdiction with a flexible constitution, according to this kind of thinking, the legislature must observe the formal rules in force in order to enact valid statutes. If it wishes to change the rules governing the formal lawmaking process, it must do so directly, by a statute enacted for that purpose, rather than by implication. At the same time, the more fundamentalist view can be taken that even examination of the formal validity of legislation exceeds the judicial power and violates the principle of separation of powers. In revolutionary France this position had substantial support, but the tendency toward giving ordinary courts the power to review the formal validity of legislation has grown stronger. The generally prevailing doctrine has arrived at this position, although it still recognizes the power of the legislature to amend the substantive provisions of a flexible constitution simply by enacting legislation inconsistent with it.

In the case of a rigid constitution, however, conflicting legislation is by definition incapable of amending constitutional provisions. A direct amending process, usually more cumbersome and difficult than the ordinary legislative process, is required. In the presence of such a constitution, a good case can be made for giving an ordinary court the power to review the substantive validity of legislation. A law that conflicts with a substantive constitutional provision, so the reasoning goes, is not really a valid law because it exceeds the legislature's power, and it should therefore not be applied by the court. This is the theoretical basis of judicial review of constitutionality in the United States, as established in the famous case of *Marbury v. Madison*; and it has also been adopted in most civil law jurisdictions in Latin America.

In general, it can be said that the experience with review by ordinary courts, even where concentrated in one supreme court, has not been encouraging. The tendency has been for the civil law judge to recoil from the responsibilities and opportunities of constitutional adjudication. The tradition is too strong, the orthodox view of the judicial function too deeply ingrained, the effects of traditional legal education and career training too limiting. Concentrated judicial review by the supreme court existed in Chile for most of the twentieth century, but by 1970 only a few statutes were found unconstitutional, and those usually in cases of minor importance. Judges have had the power of constitutional review in Japan since after World War II, but in the first three decades the Japanese supreme court found only one statute enacted by the Japanese parliament unconstitutional, and that one was expressly held not to be invalid. Examples could be multiplied.

This sort of experience, in addition to the traditional civil law distrust of ordinary judges, the force of the doctrine of separation of powers, and the desire to give decisions of unconstitutionality *erga omnes* effects, explains the decision in Austria, Germany, Italy, and Spain, among many other civil law nations, to establish separate constitutional courts. The analogy with the nineteenth-century decision to establish separate tribunals for judicial review of the legality of administrative acts is clear.

The German, Italian, and Spanish constitutional courts were established after World War II and represent the modern trend toward constitutional review in the civil law world. Although there are important differences between them, they share a number of significant characteristics. All are separate courts, distinct from all others in their respective jurisdictions. All have the exclusive power to decide on the constitutionality of legislation. In Germany, Italy, and Spain a decision by the constitutional court that a statute is unconstitutional is binding not only on the parties to the case but also on all participants in the legal process. In all three instances the character of the proceedings and the rules governing the selection and tenure of judges give the constitutional court a definitely judicial character, in contrast to the political nature of the French Constitutional Council.

Generally, the procedure is this: in an action before a civil, criminal, administrative, or other court, a party can raise a constitutional objection to a statute affecting the case. At this point the action is suspended, and the constitutional question is referred to the constitutional court for decision. When that decision is published, the original proceeding is resumed and conducted in accordance with it. If the constitutional court finds the statute constitutional, it can be applied in the proceeding; if the court rules it unconstitutional, the statute becomes invalid and cannot be applied in that specific proceeding or in any other. This procedure exemplifies the so-called incidental attack on constitutionality.

The incidental procedure, which permits a constitutional attack only in the context of a specific case or controversy, is the only one available in the system of constitutional review in the United States. In Germany, Italy, and Spain (as well as other civil law countries, including Austria, Colombia, Costa Rica, Guatemala, Mexico, Peru, and Venezuela), however, a "direct" attack is also possible. Designated official agencies of government and even individuals can bring an action before the constitutional court to test the validity of a statute, even though there is no concrete dispute involving its application. In this way the limitations inherent in the restriction to incidental review in the United States are transcended, and a hearing can be had on the abstract question of constitutionality. Even though limited by statute and decision, the direct review procedure significantly expands the availability of constitutional review beyond that available in the United States.

It is clear that by first creating separate administrative courts, and later by establishing special constitutional courts, a number of civil law nations have moved a long way toward the ideal of what civil lawyers call the *Rechtstaat*: a system of government in which the acts of agencies and officials of all kinds are subject to the principle of legality, and in which procedures are available to interested persons to test the legality of governmental action and to have an appropriate remedy when the act in question fails to pass the test. A good argument can be made that the system of reviewing the legality of administrative action in the civil law world is more efficient and effective than ours. The development of an effective system of constitutional review of legislation in civil law countries has come much later than the American system, and it is still too early to judge how it will actually work over time. But the necessary parts all seem to be there, and the possibility exists that the range of legal protection against unconstitutional legislation within the civil law world may eventually exceed that available to citizens of the United States.

In Chapter VI we described the civil law judge's relatively low status in the civil law world when compared with the prestige of the legislative and executive powers. A practical effect of the widespread adoption of constitutional review since World War II has been to increase the power and transform the stature of judges. Their new and growing preeminence is a powerful indicator of a radical transformation of the civil law tradition.

XIX

PERSPECTIVES

BEFORE SPECULATING about the future of the civil law in the next chapter, it is important to put the discussion from previous chapters into perspective. We need to correct some of the distortions that may have been caused by the selectivity, emphasis, and simplification that have necessarily characterized the prior discussion. One way the reader can acquire perspective is by further reading, and for this purpose a brief bibliography of recommended readings appears at the end of this book. The books and articles cited there themselves refer to other publications to which the still-unsatisfied reader can go. That is really the better way to go about perfecting one's understanding of the civil law tradition, and this chapter is a less satisfactory substitute.

One possible source of misunderstanding grows out of the difficulty of keeping our precise objective in mind. We have not attempted to describe any existing civil law system. Rather, we have sought to describe certain powerful historical events and currents of thought that have deeply influenced the growth of contemporary civil law systems and that give form and meaning to the legal rules, institutions, and processes that make up those systems. The precise legal rules in force differ widely from one civil law system to another. The specific solutions for typically recurring social or political problems that they embody are sometimes similar, but often they are quite different—even opposed. A transfer of land is ineffective until entered in the land register in Germany, but such a register does not even exist in Belgium. The practice of law was a divided profession in France but never in Chile. The decisory oath still exists in Italy but has been abolished in Austria. The organization, composition, and jurisdiction of courts in Spain is distinguishable in many ways from that in the Netherlands. The Mexican *amparo* is not the same thing as the Brazilian *mandado de segurança*, and both are markedly different from the Italian system of constitutional review. The legal systems and their role in society also change quite quickly and frequently because of their relation to the social and political system.

The Brazilian Supreme Federal Court works quite differently, and with different consequences for society, in 1987 and in 2017.

Examples could easily be multiplied. Indeed, at the level of concrete application of a specific rule to a specific case by a specific court in a specific proceeding, it would be hard to find two civil law systems that would operate in the same way to produce the same results. The resultant of the forces represented by the substantive rules, procedures, and institutions that come into play in the decision of a case in one nation is almost invariably different from the resultant of analogous forces in another. The emphasis here has been not on the differences but on what these legal systems have in common, on what it is that relates them to each other in a way that makes it possible to contrast them with other legal families, the products of other legal traditions.

However, there is an analogous problem in talking about the civil law tradition itself. The impact of the various components of that tradition has varied from one nation to another. Consider German legal science; it has never taken deep root in France, but the Italians have, in this sense, become more German than the Germans. Consider the ideology of the French Revolution and the effect it had on the form, style, and content of the Code Napoléon; the German Civil Code represents a conscious rejection of a number (but not all) of the premises of the French codification. Civil codes enacted since the nineteenth century show the influences of both. Consider the Roman civil law. It grew up in Italy, it was formally received in Germany, and it was gradually absorbed in France, with different consequences for each system. The extent of influence of indigenous law is another variable. In Italy, the *jus commune* was indigenous law, but in some European nations, particularly France and Germany, separate local legal customs and institutions were consciously preserved, glorified, and integrated into the new unified legal order of the state. In others, such as Spain, regional indigenous legal characteristics have been retained as locally applicable law (the *fueros* of Catalonia, Aragon, and other formerly independent kingdoms).

The age of a code is another important variable. For example, the civil codes in force in civil law jurisdictions vary in age from the Code Napoléon of 1804, still in force in France, to shiny new postwar civil codes in some nations. The problems involved in interpreting and applying very old codes are of course quite different from those encountered with very new ones. The old codes are products of a different time and do not speak to a great range of contemporary problems that are the express concern of the new code. Two principal consequences flow from the failure to modernize the old codes: one is the tendency to put some obstacles to economic and social change; the other, much more important, is the imposition of a greater burden on judicial interpretation as a progressive element in the legal process. The greater the gap between what society needs and what the code says, the greater the tendency for courts to develop new interpretations of old code provisions in order to meet the need. Judicial decisions become in fact, if not in theory, a source of law.

The actual operation of the legal order within civil law nations is thus affected both by the age of the codes in force and by the judicial response to the adequacy of old codes. In France much of the power of the old code to impede social and economic progress has been reduced by a creative judiciary. But in some civil law nations, particularly those outside Europe, old codes of the French type are applied by a judiciary that still sees itself, and is still seen by others, in the image that emerged from the French Revolution. The result is a lack of judicial response to the needs of a changing society and economy. While embracing the French style of code and the French revolutionary image of the judge and the legislator, such nations have often failed to develop the pragmatic French solution of a covertly but effectively creative judiciary.

Consequently, it is necessary to emphasize that the precise mixture of local influences and of components of the civil law tradition, the precise timing of such important events as the enactment of the codes in force, and the precise extent of French, Italian, and German influence on the legal process, varies widely throughout the civil law world. This adds another series of variables to the differing substantive rules of law, legal institutions, and legal processes. Civil law nations share the civil law tradition, but they share it to different degrees.

Another possible source of distortion in this account of the civil law tradition is the necessarily selective nature of the discussion. We have examined only a few readily identifiable characteristics of this tradition, and although these are probably the most important, we should not forget that they are not the only ones. For example, we have not discussed in any detail the strength of the royal tradition in Europe or the survival, beyond the time of the French Revolution, of a number of institutions and attitudes whose origins are traceable primarily to the absolute monarchies. We have not lingered over the proposition, for which there is a good deal of historical evidence, that nations once subject to absolute rule have found it easy to slip back into authoritarian regimes in one form or another. We have not considered the fact that the executive branches of all European governments were originally creations of the monarchies, and we have avoided discussing the importance of these origins in understanding the peculiar ways in which legal controls over administrative actions have evolved in the civil law tradition. We have not commented on the growing professionalization of government administration, or on the tendency for it to become a distinctive career, often (particularly in Germany) dominated by lawyers. Many other examples could be cited, for we have only touched the surface in this book.

The legal tradition is a part of the culture, a very old, deeply rooted, firmly held part. The relations between basic legal ideas and similarly profound social, economic, and political attitudes are extremely close and extremely complex. The law both draws meaning from and supplies meaning to the rest of the culture, and it is inseparable from it. We have tried to understand some of these interrelationships, but it would be a mistake to assume that we have exhausted the subject.

From time to time certain aspects of the civil law tradition have been criticized expressly or by implication. In particular, it has been suggested that there is something excessive about the emphasis on a sharp separation of powers; that the effort to make the law judge-proof is both futile and, in the long run, socially undesirable; that the quest for certainty has become both a romantic form of snark hunting and a meaningless, catchword argument, available to support any position; that the role of the legislature has become bloated out of all proportion, far beyond the ability of that institution to meet the demands placed on it; that the premises and methods of German legal science have isolated the law from the problems of the society it is supposed to serve while perpetuating a set of socioeconomic assumptions that are no longer valid, if they ever were; and that the civil law is dominated by a misdirected scholarly tradition, diverting the great potential influence and the enormous energy, creativity, and cultivated intelligence of civil law teacher-scholars into essentially arid pursuits.

These are not merely the reactions of an American lawyer to the prominently exotic features of an inadequately understood foreign legal tradition. Such criticisms are not original to common lawyers. Civil law scholars themselves, critically examining their own law and calling for its reform, make them all. This brings us to a third possible source of misunderstanding: the assumption that the civil law tradition today is both monolithic and static. It is neither.

What we have described as the civil law tradition is, first of all, a set of dominant influences and attitudes, those that stand out among a variety of competing historical and intellectual forces, the ones that have emerged most prominently from the competition for acceptance. The model of the positivistic state that emerged from the thought of the seventeenth and eighteenth centuries and from the revolution represented a victory for its adherents over the strongly held views of natural law proponents and the advocates of other forms of social and political organization. The Roman civil law—*jus commune*—competed with native legal traditions for dominance of the unified national legislation of France and Germany. German legal science was only one set of attitudes about the objectives and methods of legal scholarship and the nature and functions of the legal order. At every point in the history of the civil law tradition a variety of forces have been at work. This is particularly true today. Every aspect of the law is under critical examination by legal scholars, who question not only specific rules, institutions, and processes but also the basic components of the legal tradition that give the positive legal order form and meaning. The orthodoxy of the time is constantly under attack. We have seen only the most prominent and durable components of a pluralistic legal tradition.

Just as the civil law tradition is far from monolithic, so is it in constant transition. The dominant characteristics described in this book represent only one stage in a process that began nearly twenty-five centuries ago and can be expected to continue long into the future. The Roman civil law alone has passed through many phases—preclassical and classical law, Justinian's *Corpus Juris Civilis*, the contributions of the glossators and the commentators, the writings of the humanists, the French codification, the theories of Savigny and the historical school, German legal science, and the BGB. And this is only one strand in the fabric of the civil law tradition. The canon law began as a law of and for the Roman Catholic Church, grew in spiritual jurisdiction as the church's power spread, and eventually was extended when the ecclesiastical tribunals acquired temporal jurisdiction; it made an important contribution to the *jus commune*, and, after the Reformation, disappeared as a major continuing influence on the development of the civil law tradition. The commercial law began as a group of customary practices created by pragmatic merchants to meet their own needs. Eventually commercial law and commercial courts were nationalized, becoming a part of the official apparatus of the state, together with separate commercial codes. Today the separate commercial courts are disappearing, and there is a similar trend with respect to separate commercial codes. Nowadays commerce and commercial law are becoming more international, necessitating adoption of new, hybrid legal regulations.

As we will see more fully in Chapter XX, there has been a gradually accelerating movement away from the extremes of the revolutionary model of the legal process. The extension of the power of statutory interpretation by the ordinary courts was an important early step, supported by the growing practice of publishing and citing judicial opinions. The creation of tribunals to review the legality of administrative action was another. Even where such tribunals were historically a part of the administration, as in France, they now look and act like courts. Despite rejection of the doctrine of stare decisis, the practice of courts is to decide similar cases similarly, in much the same way as do common law courts. More recently the adoption of rigid constitutions, filling the gap left by the rejection of natural law as a check on the legislature, has been accompanied by a variety of devices to keep legislation within constitutional limits. There has been a substantial shift of power from legislature to court (and also from legislature to executive, but that is another topic), eroding the ideal of legislative supremacy. The powers of courts to review both the legality of administrative action and the constitutionality of legislative action, and to interpret statutes, undermine the dogma of strict separation of powers. A legal process designed to make the law judge-proof has become steadily more judicialized, and today the rate of judicialization is accelerating throughout the civil law world.

German legal science has been the object of satire, ridicule, and direct attack by legal thinkers in Germany and elsewhere from the time of its emergence. More recently, and particularly since World War II, its critics have begun to have more effect. There is a growing group of scholars who call for a fresh approach to legal scholarship. Some of them demand rejection of all that legal science has accomplished. Others treat legal science as a valid but spent phase in the evolution of the civil law tradition; they wish to preserve the gains made by it, particularly the provision of order and system in the law, and build on them. All agree that the purity of legal science—its rejection of everything considered nonlegal—has had the effect of separating law from the life of the society whose problems should be its basic concern. This social, economic, and political agnosticism has cut the law off from the rest of the culture and has made lawyers less and less relevant to social needs. At the same time, the social and economic assumptions that are embodied in the abstract conceptions of legal science seem to some critics to conflict with the contents of modern constitutions and the programs of modern governments. The argument is made that exaltation of the private legal relation, the subjective right, and the private juridical act (described in Chapter XI) perpetuates an individualistic, nineteenth-century form of economic and social Darwinism, impeding governmental redistribution of power, status, and wealth, and makes the law and lawyers, often unconsciously, into reactionary forces. Such criticisms have special force and relevance in developing nations within the civil law world, particularly in Latin America in the 1970s and onward. There a number of legal scholars have argued that the legal process was lagging behind the rest of the culture, inadequate as a vehicle for economic and social change, sometimes inherently opposed to such change, and with increasing frequency irrelevant to it. These critical scholars largely won what two observers called the "palace wars" and have successfully promoted a more modern vision of the legal process.

These kinds of dissatisfaction with legal science have been reinforced by a shift in the legal order's center of gravity. The bastion of legal science has traditionally been private law, and particularly Roman civil law. Until recently, the civil code has served something like a constitutional function in civil law systems, providing a scheme of private rights that it was the primary business of government to protect and enforce. General principles and general theories of law, derived primarily from the materials of private law, dominated the legislative and judicial processes. As a result, the civil code and the doctrinal work of civil lawyers furnished the ideological fuel of the legal process. But with the adoption of modern rigid constitutions embodying new social and economic conceptions, and with the establishment of judicial review of the constitutionality of legislation in important civil law nations, the legal center of gravity has begun to undergo what promises to be a dramatic shift from civil code to constitution, from private law to public law, from ordinary court to constitutional court, from legislative positivism to constitutional principle and the human rights primacy. The provisions of constitutions and human rights treaties are an alternative source of general principles; they offer an alternative set of notions to guide judges in the interpretation and application of statutes, including the provisions of civil codes. The power of constitutional or other courts to find statutes invalid *erga omnes* lends great authority to constitutional provisions. In legal systems where a modern rigid constitution coupled with judicial review confronts a strong tradition of legal science, as is the case in Germany, Italy, and Spain today, a fundamental readjustment of the legal process is under way.

With these perspectives on the variety, complexity, and dynamism of the civil law tradition in mind, we turn at last to a brief consideration of the most fascinating perspective of all: the comparative. Most amateurs of comparative law will look impatiently through this book for the answers to two great questions: What is the difference between the common law and the civil law? Which is better? Each of these questions provides an appropriate topic for another book. Neither can be answered here, but a few comments on each are in order.

First, what is the difference? Many comparisons between aspects of the civil law and the common law have been made or implied throughout this discussion, often on the assumption that readers have a general familiarity with their own legal tradition. Readers have thus already acquired some notions about fundamental differences between the two legal traditions. But unless they have an unusually thorough and sophisticated knowledge of the common law, they are ill equipped for thorough comparative consideration even of those matters that were selected for discussion in this book. And it is hardly necessary to add that any sort of adequate comparison would require the consideration of a multitude of topics that we have not discussed at all. This book does not answer the question "What is the difference?" It merely indicates what some of the differences are and describes something of their origins and their significance.

Which is better? At one level this is a foolish question. It is like asking whether the French language is superior to the English language. Better for whom? Surely no one would suggest that the Italians would be better off with the common law tradition or the Americans with the civil law. The law is rooted in the culture and history, and it responds, within cultural limits, to the specific demands of a given society in a given time and place. It is, at bottom, a historically determined process by which certain social problems are perceived, formulated, and resolved. Substitution of one legal tradition for another is neither possible nor desirable. This does not mean that traditions are closed universes. Professional legal education at the universities was a fundamental feature of the civil law tradition received in the United States in the nineteenth century. The awareness of the central role of judges in shaping the law is a central part of the common law tradition that many civil law systems received in late twentieth century.

At a different level the question becomes more respectable: To what extent does the legal tradition respond to the demands legitimately made on it by a given society? To what extent does the tradition impede the realization of worthy political, economic, and social objectives? Are civil law nations more adequately served by their legal systems than are common law nations? A moment's reflection on such questions produces others. By which criteria can we make this kind of judgment? How does one evaluate degrees of satisfaction of complex social, economic, and political demands? How can one even determine clearly what such demands are? There may be satisfactory ways of answering these questions, but it is obvious that they extend far beyond the range of this book.

We can, however, recognize the subtlety and complexity of the differences between the two legal traditions and come to understand how a misunderstanding of those differences can affect all forms and phases of international dealings. The easy judgments, the careless assumptions that people in both traditions commonly make about foreign legal systems, are a constant source of misunderstanding and irritation. They get in the way of international negotiations. They cripple foreign aid programs. They limit the effectiveness of cultural exchange. They misdirect effort and misallocate resources. A person who would not think of going to a foreign nation without some understanding of its history, politics, language, and literature will almost invariably arrive in total ignorance of one of the oldest and most important elements of its culture: its legal tradition.

It is unlikely, although it might be desirable, that thoughtful comparative lawyers will regularly be included in the teams that formulate foreign policies and programs at various governmental and private levels within the common law world. It is only slightly less unlikely that they will regularly be called on to participate in the elaboration and execution of such policies and programs. One reason is that there are too few of them, although that problem might be remedied if the demand existed. But the main reason is that the demand is not there. Comparative lawyers have failed to sensitize others, lawyers and nonlawyers alike, to the realization that something important is missing from the array of expertise customarily brought to bear on relations with nations in the civil law world.

What is missing is the realization that there is something out there in the civil law world that is important and different. It is more than a set of different legal rules. It is not summed up in stereotypes about civil law codes and common law judicial decisions. It is subtler than that, and more pervasive. It has historical, political, social—in a word, cultural—dimensions. Anyone, lawyer or nonlawyer, who wants to understand Europe and Latin America (or, for that matter, the civil law nations of the Middle East, Asia, and Africa) should become familiar with the civil law tradition.

XX

THE FUTURE OF THE CIVIL
LAW TRADITION

W<small>E HAVE</small> seen the image of a legal system that emerged from the revolution and legal science: one that contemplated such things as a legal universe inhabited only by the individual and the state; legislative supremacy; a rigorous separation of the judicial from the legislative and administrative powers; a narrowly defined and uncreative judicial role; the denial of stare decisis; the primacy of the civil code and of civil law scholarship; a highly developed and coherent conceptual structure; and a constant preoccupation with certainty. We have also seen a number of the ways in which this nineteenth-century model has been subjected to criticism and erosion in modern civil law nations. In this chapter, we look further at the process of erosion and describe what appears to be a fundamental transformation taking place in the civil law tradition. That transformation is symbolized in part by the decline of civil codes, in part by the rise of constitutions, and in part by the growth of European federalism. These associated tendencies toward the "decodification," "constitutionalization," and "federalization" of the civil law tradition seem to be irreversible. They also seem to have substantial momentum, indicating that they will continue to affect the development of the civil law tradition in the future. We begin with decodification.

"Special legislation," in the civil law world, refers to laws that grow up around the codes and regulate topics that articles of the codes themselves treat. That there are large bodies of special legislation supplementing the civil codes is easily verified by a look at any major civil law jurisdiction. Some of this legislation merely elucidates matters governed by code provisions, completing and clarifying the original code design. But the great bulk of it does something quite different: it sets up special legal regimes, "microsystems of law," that differ ideologically from the code and in this sense are incompatible with it. Labor law provides a familiar and significant example. In the classic civil codes, the "labor relation" is treated as merely one variety of contracts between individuals exercising liberty of contract;

labor contracts are not greatly different from other contracts, except that here money is exchanged for labor rather than for goods or for real estate. But in modern civil law nations, just as in the United States, the central players are big labor and management, not private individuals, and government's regulations are very important. Labor legislation has a variety of objectives quite unfamiliar to the regime of the civil codes: the welfare and safety of workers, industrial peace and productivity, regulation of the internal affairs and public accountability of labor unions and employers' associations, and so forth. Whereas the traditional civil codes left it to private individuals to pursue their own interests, with the state acting largely in the restricted role of a referee, enforcing the rules of the game, the new provisions embody policy choices and are designed to further specific social objectives. The microsystem of labor law is thus fundamentally different in approach and technique from the code provisions for labor contracts.

The labor law example illustrates another aspect of special laws. They are not the agreed-on products of tranquil reflection by legislators expressing a substantial consensus; they are instead compromises worked out between special interests (here labor and management) in the legislative arena. Legislators of course affect the outcome, but the political and economic power of the partisan interests and the quality of the expertise and advocacy that these interests bring to bear give them a dominant voice. (According to an Italian scholar, the classic civil code provision that "the contract is law for the parties" has been reversed in the case of special legislation to "the law is the contract of the parties.") Because special interests are special, they tend to be interested in their own problems and to have divergent concerns. One result is that special legislation is heterogeneous, diverse, and pluralistic, in contrast to the formal and ideological coherence of the civil code. It is closely associated with public policy and cannot claim to come from reason or a long tradition.

Important microsystems of statutory law have grown up on a variety of civil code topics: urban leases, agrarian leases, intellectual property, the formation and conduct of companies, and the marketing and trading of company securities, to name just a few. Even family law, considered for so many years as a bulwark of stability, is now subject to ideological discussions and policy decisions. Such laws are not mere supplements to the code; they are successful competitors to it. (Indeed, it has become common to call such microsystems "codes"—e.g., the French Code du Travail—and thus to formalize their rival status. But the name of code does not make it more stable). Cases are decided according to the provisions of the special legislation, not civil code provisions. As the amount of special legislation grows, the code becomes more and more a body of residual law to be turned to only if some more specific provision of special legislation cannot be found. If we recall that one function of a carefully drafted, substantively coherent civil code was to provide certainty in the law (see Chapter VIII), it is apparent that much special legislation impairs the quest for that kind of certainty.

Parallel to the growth of statutory microsystems is the growth of equally important systems of judge-made law. The law of torts under French-style codes is a prominent example, to which we have previously referred. The code provisions are so rudimentary and so empty of substance that judges have had to create the applicable law on a case-by-case basis. The effective law of torts is accordingly not found in the code but outside it, in the widely published, consulted, and cited decisions of the courts. Unlike the legislative process, which proceeds sporadically and in substantial increments, the judicial process is gradual and accretive. Over time, the significance attached to facts and the attitudes of judges toward proper outcomes imperceptibly change, and the law also changes. No French or German judge deciding an automobile collision case today can truly ignore the mass phenomenon of the automobile, the inevitability of automobile collisions, or the existence of public liability insurance. As such considerations creep into judicial decisions, the law changes in ways that are analogous to the changes introduced by much special legislation. The new law is fundamentally different in outlook from the premises and objectives of the code.

The number and importance of the microsystems created by special legislation and by judges help us to understand something that often puzzles common lawyers: why civil law jurisdictions—in particular France, with the oldest civil code still in force—retain their old civil codes rather than replace them with modern ones. In the case of France, one partial answer is that the French are proud of and sentimentally attached to the Code Napoléon. It is a cultural monument. There is bound to be some resistance to proposals to replace it. Even so, there were two attempts at wholesale revision in the twentieth century. The first almost literally came to nothing. The second began bravely, in 1945, with a distinguished commission headed by a respected scholar, and with lots of fanfare, confident speeches, periodic published reports, and partial drafts. Gradually, however, the commission subsided and dropped from public view. Eventually it stopped work entirely and was quietly abolished. Since then the effort has been to amend the code piecemeal, and by now more than a third of the original provisions have been revised, replaced, or simply repealed. The process is done in such a way as to preserve, rather than replace, the monument. The original numbering of articles in the code has been retained, so that the new matter follows the old organization. Even this process has, after a period of fairly rapid activity, begun to slow. Meanwhile the large body of legislative and judicial microsystems of law outside the code remains substantially unaffected by the code revision process.

The reason for this is that the civil code is a coherent expression of a particular ideology, which was described in Chapter V. The microsystems of special legislation outside the code, however, express their own attitudes and values, which are often inconsistent with those of the code. The piecemeal process of revision just described has dealt with the easy parts, with those aspects of the code that can be adapted without undue difficulty to contemporary life. Any attempt to incorporate the body of special legislation into the code faces insuperable problems, of which the most significant may be that the microsystems themselves are often incompatible in outlook. They are also voluminous, and to incorporate them into a civil code would blow the code up to an unmanageable size. The practical solution is to abandon the project for a new civil code and to leave in place the old one, with its historical dignity and utility as residual law. It is significant that the civil codes of the twentieth century were adopted in the Soviet Union and other socialist nations, where socialist ideology and authoritarian regimes provided the necessary unifying and propelling force; in Fascist Italy, where a quite different authoritarian regime and ideology were at work; and in Greece, where something was badly needed to replace the ninth-century Basilica as the primary civil law source. More recently Portugal, Cuba, and Peru also published new civil codes more adapted to modern society or changing ideologies. Other countries have modified substantial parts of their civil codes.

The decline in legislative supremacy, on which we have already commented in Chapter V, has recently taken on an important additional dimension. Recall that legislatures can delegate lawmaking power to the executive, who then, by "legislative decree," actually legislates. This practice accelerated at an extraordinary rate throughout the civil law world in the second part of the twentieth century, for reasons that seem to reflect a growing inability of representative parliaments to fulfill the roles assigned to them by nineteenth-century ideology. Much contemporary legislation is thus the product not of a popularly elected parliament but of a less public process conducted within the offices of the executive. What some observers consider the next logical step occurred in France with adoption of the constitution of the Fifth Republic, in 1958. The legislative jurisdiction of parliament, previously unlimited, was sharply reduced by transferring a substantial portion of it to the executive, and a special organ, the Constitutional Council, was established to ensure that parliament did not exceed its restricted jurisdiction. Executives exercise their legislative jurisdiction simply by issuing "regulations." To give some idea of the effect of this constitutional alteration, a new French code of civil procedure was adopted by such a regulation. It was not necessary for the parliament to repeal the old code or consent to the new one. The executive regulation alone had the necessary repealing and enacting effect.

A further aspect of the decline of legislatures (and of legislation, including the codes) is found in the growth of public administrations. The people who hold positions in the public administrations interpret laws, issue rules, and make decisions. They form the largest branch of government, which far exceeds in personnel and in volume of business the combined judicial and legislative branches. It is true that administrative officials are in theory subject to the law and cannot legally exceed or misuse the authority given to them. But the same is true of judges, and we have seen how ineffective legislative control is over judicial interpretation. In interpreting and applying laws, issuing regulations, and deciding disputes, administrative officials have an irreducible space for incremental lawmaking. In France and in nations following the French model, alleged excesses and misuses of administrative power are judged not by the legislature or by ordinary judges but by members of the public administration itself, sitting in a council of state. The council has developed its own body of law, largely independent of legislation, to guide it. In this way administrative law has become detached from its legislative source. It is a rival law that often affects the lives of citizens more directly and profoundly than legislation or litigation in ordinary courts. In fact, administrative litigation has grown much more rapidly than the work of ordinary courts.

Some civil law scholars have compared the outcome of the process of decodification and the decline of legislative authority to the situation in Europe before the revolution (discussed in Chapter III). The law, they say, is once again uncertain, complex, and particular, and thus at odds with the needs for certainty, simplicity, and uniformity. Others see the movement in less alarming terms: the evolution from a monocentric to a polycentric legal system is perceived as a normal result of the movement toward a more complex, pluralistic, and polycentric society. If laws have a shorter half-life and become more quickly antiquated, this is simply a normal reflection of the increasing pace of social change. In a consumer-oriented, "disposable" society, individual laws, or prevailing interpretations of them, also become disposable.

While legislatures and codes have declined throughout the civil law world, the practice of treating constitutions as the supreme sources of law has grown, as has the range of opportunities to challenge the constitutionality of legislative or other official acts. In Europe the phenomenon has taken the form of new constitutions that provide for the establishment of special tribunals with the power of judicial review—for example, the Austrian, German, and Italian constitutional "courts," the Spanish constitutional "tribunal," and the French Constitutional Council. In Latin America and Japan, influenced by the example of the United States, the power of review is generally lodged in national supreme courts, which have long been theoretically capable of a form of judicial review. Nevertheless, some Latin American countries, like Colombia, Guatemala and Chile, preferred the European model of constitutional court. What is new is the growing extent to which that power of judicial review is exercised.

In no civil law nation is constitutional review exactly like the review familiar to us, nor are any two review procedures within the civil law world identical. Through the Colombian "popular action" and the German "constitutional complaint," for example, people in those nations have a direct access to judicial review that we do not enjoy. The French Constitutional Council, preserving the appearance of a separation of powers, is a nonjudicial body that can prevent the promulgation of an unconstitutional law but can do nothing about one that has already been promulgated. Additional variations are described in Chapter XVIII.

Despite these variations, the movement toward constitutionalism displays a number of common features. For one thing, the new constitutionalism has prominently sought to guarantee and to expand individual rights: rights to civil and criminal due process of law; to equality; to freedom of association, movement, expression, and belief; and to education, work, health care, and economic security. The "old" individual rights that were an objective of revolution and that received their "constitutional" protection in the civil codes—rights of personality, property, and liberty of contract—have to a large extent been achieved and solidified in the work of ordinary courts quietly applying the traditional sources and methods of law. The constitutions are the sites of the new individual rights, and the clash of constitutional litigation is the medium of their definition and enforcement. The rise of constitutionalism is in this sense an additional form of decodification: the civil codes no longer serve a constitutional function. As we have previously remarked, that function has moved from the most private of private law sources, the civil code, to the most public of public law sources, the constitution.

It is clear that the new constitutionalism involves a significant transfer of power and prestige to judges. Admittedly, these judges are not those who staff the ordinary courts (although ordinary judges have also received a portion of this new power), but the very distinction has lost most of its importance. To the ordinary citizen, and to a growing number of scholars, constitutional court decisions are the work of judges who have the power to declare legislation void. There is only a limited and rapidly decreasing nostalgia for legislative supremacy, for the separation of powers, and for a limited judicial role in the legal process. Constitutional decisions are often glamorous, attracting the attention of the public and the media in a way that the decisions of ordinary courts seldom do. Indeed, the tradition is for ordinary judges to avoid excitement, to act as anonymous functionaries obediently applying the legislative will. Constitutional judges, in contrast, are often personalities; their votes and opinions are news, the subject of public debate. Their decisions exhibit a drift away from the conceptual structure and the style of traditional civil law scholarship, employing terms and ideas unfamiliar to legal science (hence they are said to be unscientific, which, in this sense, they are). The loss of "certainty" that follows from decodification is thus magnified by the loss of the logical structure of legal science. In short, every aspect of the traditional image of the legal process described in Chapter XII is impaired by the growth of constitutionalism.

The development of the European Union and the legal apparatus of the European Convention on Human Rights add exponentially to the breakdown of the old system. The European Court of Justice can set aside national laws that conflict with Community law; European law, like federal law under the U.S. Constitution, is supreme. National courts are required to refuse to apply national laws that conflict with Community law. They must refer questions of interpretation of Community law to the European Court. National laws in violation of the European Convention on Human Rights can be challenged before the European Commission and the Court of Human Rights. Both the internal and the external sovereignty of the state have been decisively reduced. Internally, the growth of human rights and the recognition of group and class interests transfer sovereignty from the state to individuals, groups, and classes; externally, the growing authority of the European law and the European Convention on Human Rights transfers sovereignty from the state to international bodies.

Contemplating these events, some observers draw an analogy with the medieval period, when Europe was united by the Roman civil law—canon law, *jus commune*. They see the law of the European Union and the Convention on Human Rights as the foundation of a new European *jus commune*, based on common culture and common interests, after centuries of exaggerated glorification of the nation-state. The fact that Great Britain, the mother country of the common law tradition, became a member of the European Union and a party to the convention suggested to them the possibility, indeed the necessity, of a rapprochement of the civil law and common law traditions. The present situation is more ambiguous because of the British decision to withdraw from the European Union. Nevertheless, it appears likely that Great Britain will remain in the Council of Europe and that the European human rights law will continue in force in Great Britain.

Although there have been difficulties and disappointments, European integration is perhaps a manifestation of the more general phenomenon of globalization, which entails a generalization of exchanges that have weakened national frontiers. Many contracts are now international, frequently drafted by international law firms. International courts of arbitration are increasingly used. In a certain way, the law has weakened its relation to the national state. Is it the dawn of a new era of *jus commune* beyond the frontiers or Europe? In any case, globalization is a lively and significant force with important consequences for contemporary civil law (and common law) systems.

Legal change, of course, is inevitable, and we have described significant changes in the civil law tradition in this book. A thoughtful observer who described the civil law tradition in 1800 could not possibly have anticipated or perceived the significance of features we have placed at the center of that tradition. Nor is the legal tradition we have depicted here the same as the one displayed in the first (1969) edition of this book.

A tradition is, by definition, something that has continuity and seems opposed to innovation, to change. Do changes in the civil law tradition indicate its decline? Clearly not. As Heraclitus observed, rivers flow, and we never bathe twice in the same waters. Although the tradition changes, it follows a pattern; there is a path dependency. The forces that alter societies necessarily affect legal systems, but in ways that are determined by previous experiences. Change is a sign of continued life.

Despite the apparently dramatic impact of movements toward decodification, constitutionalism, and federalism, it would be inaccurate to assume that the civil law tradition is losing its vitality. On the contrary, it may be more alive than ever. Just as it has been necessary in this book to speak of earlier major developments—the different lives and ages of Roman law; the vicissitudes of canon law; the independent rise, evolution, and eventual absorption of commercial law; the earthshaking events of the revolution; and the extraordinary intellectual structure achieved by legal science—so one day it will be necessary to add a sixth to the catalog of civil law subtraditions. We do not know what it will be called or how future observers will describe it. We can, however, be reasonably confident that this oldest and most influential of the Western legal traditions has entered a new and dynamic stage of its development.

RECOMMENDED READINGS

ON THE CIVIL LAW GENERALLY

Mary Ann Glendon, Michael W. Gordon, and Christopher Osakwe. *Comparative Legal Traditions in a Nutshell*. St. Paul, MN: West Publishing, 1982.
This volume includes a good discussion of *The Civil Law Tradition* by Professor Glendon.

John Henry Merryman and David S. Clark. *Comparative Law: Western European and Latin American Legal Systems—Cases and Materials*. Indianapolis: Bobbs-Merrill, 1978.

John Henry Merryman, David S. Clark, and John O. Haley. *Comparative Law: Historical Development of the Civil Law Tradition in Europe, Latin America, and East Asia*. San Francisco: LexisNexis, 2010.
Like the books by Schlesinger and by Von Mehren and Gordley (see below), these two books are intended for use in law school courses. They are unique, however, for their broad historical and geographical scope.

Lawrence Friedman and Rogelio Pérez-Perdomo, eds. *Legal Culture in the Age of Globalization: Latin America and Latin Europe*. Palo Alto, CA: Stanford University Press, 2003.
This is a collective volume on the transformations of law and legal cultures of Argentina, Brazil, Chile, Colombia, France, Italy, Mexico, and Venezuela, as well as several comparative studies.

Rudolph B. Schlesinger. *Comparative Law: Cases-Text-Materials*. 4th ed. Mineola, NY: Foundation Press, 1980.

Arthur Taylor von Mehren and James Russell Gordley. *The Civil Law System: An Introduction to the Comparative Study of Law*. Boston: Little, Brown, 1977.
Schlesinger, as well as Von Mehren and Gordley, have prepared their books for use in law school courses, and the material is likely to baffle those who are unaccustomed to law school textbooks. Schlesinger's is the easier of the two and therefore the more useful for the general reader. Both works focus exclusively on French and German law.

Konrad Zweigert and Hein Kötz. *Comparative Law*. 3rd ed. Oxford: Clarendon Press, 1998.

Recommended Readings

Roman Law

F. H. Lawson. *A Common Lawyer Looks at the Civil Law.* Ann Arbor: University of Michigan Law School, 1953.

This delightful book consists of a set of lectures whose principal topic is the influence of Roman law on contemporary civil law. In addition, the author illuminates many other aspects of the civil law tradition with style, wit, and insight. Essential reading.

Aldo Schiavone. *The Invention of Law in the West.* Cambridge, MA: Harvard University Press, 2012.

This is a top scholarly book on the history of Roman law and its meaning for Western civilization.

Peter Stein. *Roman Law in European History.* Cambridge: Cambridge University Press, 1999.

An updated, complete, and short treatment of the subject.

Canon Law

A General Survey of Events, Sources, Persons, and Movements in Continental Legal History. Boston: Little, Brown, 1912.

Part IX is a twenty-page discussion of canon law in European legal history.

John Henry Wigmore. *A Panorama of the World's Legal Systems.* Washington, DC: Washington Law Book Company, 1928.

Chapter XIV of this illustrated survey is devoted to canon law.

Constant van de Wiel. *History of Canon Law.* Leuven, Belgium: Peeters Press, 1991.

Commercial Law

William Mitchell. *An Essay on the Early History of the Law Merchant.* Cambridge: Cambridge University Press, 1904.

Mitchell's is the classical book on the history of commercial law.

Vito Piergiovanni, ed. *From Lex Mercatoria to Commercial Law.* Berlin: Duncker & Humboldto, 2005.

A collection of scholarly essays on the subject of commercial law.

The Role of Judges

John P. Dawson. *The Oracles of the Law.* Ann Arbor: University of Michigan Law School, 1968.

This book describes in rich detail the development of the judicial traditions in Rome, England, France, and Germany from early times to the twentieth century. Although the prose style is eminently readable, this book may prove heavy going for the amateur of comparative law; but it is worth the effort.

Recommended Readings

Neal Tate and Torbjorn Vallinder, eds. *The Global Expansion of the Judicial Power*. New York: New York University Press, 1995.
An important reader on the increased importance of judges in present time.

Gretchen Helmke and Julio Ríos-Figueroa, eds. *Courts in Latin America*. Cambridge: Cambridge University Press, 2011.
An excellent reader on the new role of supreme or constitutional courts in Latin America.

Lawyers

Richard Abel and Philip Lewis, eds. *Civil Law Systems*. Vol. 3 of *Lawyers of the World*. Berkeley: University of California Press, 1988.

David Clark. "Comparing the Work and Organization of Lawyers Worldwide: The Persistence of Legal Traditions." In *Lawyers' Practice and Ideals: A Comparative View*, edited by John Barceló III and Roger Camton. New York: Kluwer Law International, 1999.

Rogelio Pérez-Perdomo. *Latin American Lawyers*. Palo Alto, CA: Stanford University Press, 2006.

On Procedural Law

Adhémar Esmein. *A History of Continental Criminal Procedure with Special Reference to France*. Translated by John Simpson. Boston: Little, Brown, 1913.
This is a classical book on the history of criminal procedure in Continental Europe.

John A. Jolowicz. *On Civil Procedure*. Cambridge: Cambridge University Press, 2000.
A good treatment of recent changes in comparative perspective.

ON THE LAW OF SPECIFIC NATIONS OR AREAS

In addition to the works listed below, useful brief descriptions of national legal systems may be found in volume 1 of the *International Encyclopedia of Comparative Law*. Tübingen: J. C. B. Mohr; The Hague: Mouton.

Herbert Kritzer, ed. *Legal Systems of the World: A Political, Social and Cultural Encyclopedia*. Santa Barbara, CA: ABC-CLIO, 2002.

France

René David. *French Law: Its Structure, Sources, and Methodology*. Translated by Michael Kindred. Baton Rouge: Louisiana State University Press, 1972.
This excellent book by an eminent French scholar comprehensively surveys the French legal system in a readable and authoritative style. Essential reading.

Recommended Readings

F. H. Lawson, E. A. Anton, and L. Neville Brown, eds. *Amos & Walton's Introduction to French Law*. 3rd ed. Oxford: Clarendon Press, 1967.
A survey of French private law, with a good (though brief) systemic and historical introduction.

Germany

E. J. Cohn. *Manual of German Law*. Vol. 1. Dobbs Ferry, NY: Oceana Publications, 1968.
Chapters 1 and 2 of this excellent work provide brief introductions to the German legal system and to the general part of the civil law.

Norbert Horn, Hein Kötz, and Hans G. Leser. *German Private and Commercial Law: An Introduction*. Translated by Tony Weir. Oxford: Clarendon Press, 1982.
The first few chapters of this readable and authoritative work provide a historical and systemic overview of German law.

Italy

Mauro Cappelletti, John Henry Merryman, and Joseph M. Perillo. *The Italian Legal System: An Introduction*. Stanford, CA: Stanford University Press, 1967.
The first work in English on the Italian legal system, now somewhat out of date.

Jeffrey S. Lena and Ugo Mattei, eds. *Introduction to Italian Law*. New York: Kluwer Law International, 2002.
This useful book contains articles on the Italian legal system by a number of Italian scholars.

Alessandra De Luca and Alessandro Simoni, eds. *Fundamentals of Italian Law*. Milan: Giuffrè, 2014.
A recent collective analysis of Italian law.

Mexico

Guillermo Floris Margadant S. *An Introduction to the History of Mexican Law*. Dobbs Ferry, NY: Oceana Publications, 1983.
As the title indicates, this work by a respected Mexican scholar emphasizes history but also contains incidental information on the legal system.

Zamora, Stephen. *Mexican Law*. Oxford: Oxford University Press, 2004.
A comprehensive treatment of the Mexican legal system.

Brazil

Fabiano Defenti and Welber Barrel. *Introduction to Brazilian Law*. Alphen aan den Rijn, The Netherlands: Kluwer, 2017.

Latin America

Matthew C. Mirow. *Latin American Law: A History of Private Law and Institutions in Spanish America*. Austin: University of Texas Press, 2004.

Recommended Readings

Ángel Oquendo. *Latin American Law*. New York: Foundation Press, 2006.

An up-to-date reader on changes in the Latin American legal systems specially designed for teaching the subject in American law schools.

Kenneth L. Karst. *Latin American Legal Institutions: Problems for Comparative Study*. Los Angeles: UCLA Latin American Center, 1966.

Although intended for use in law school courses and now quite old, this book contains a wealth of fascinating material and is highly accessible to nonlawyers.

INDEX

Absolute rights, 76
Absolute sovereignty, 21–22
Academic lawyers, 110–112
Accusatorial system, 129–130
Administrative courts, 90–91, 113
Administrative jurisdiction, 90–91, 96
Administrative law, 94, 99, 138
Administrative regulations, 24
Administrative review, 136–137
Advocates, 108–109
Age of Reason, 17
Agrarian law, 100
Algeria, 4
Allgemeiner Teil, 71
Amalfi, 14
American law school, 62, 65, 81
Amparo, 55, 125
Antifeudalism, 18
Appeal, 123–124
Appellate courts, 40, 123
Aristocracies, 16. *See also* Judicial
  aristocracy
Aristocracy of the robe, 16
"Articles of proof," 118
Astreinte, 55, 125
Austria: administrative jurisdiction
  and, 91; civil code, 45; civil pro-
  ceedings and, 116; natural law and
  judicial interpretation, 45; revision
  and, 124
Autonomy. *See* Private autonomy

Bar associations, 108–109
Baronial system, 110–111
Basilica, 9
Beccaria, Cesare, 127–128
Belgium, 91
Bodin, Jean, 20
Bologna, 9–10
Brazil, 55
British Empire, 4
Bürgerliches Gesetzbuch (BGB), 53
Byzantium, 8

California, 27, 28, 33
Canon law, 11–14, 149
Case method, 62, 65, 68, 81
Cassation, 39–41
Castile, 130
Certainty, 48–50, 52, 84
Chancellors, 50–51
Chancery courts, 50–51
Chile, 142
China, 4
Civil code(s): amending, 157–158;
  civil law systems and, 27; in common
  law systems, 33; constitutionalism
  and, 161; development in France,
  28–31; development in Germany,
  13; historical overview, 11–12; law
  of the general part and, 80–81; legal
  scholars and, 58, 59, 60; the public
  law-private law distinction and, 95;
  special legislation and, 155–158;
  variety in, 146–147
Civil contempt, 54–55
Civil juries, 115, 122
Civil law: as a component of private law,
  101–102; general part of, 70–81;
  modern dominance over commercial
  law, 103; subject matter of, 70; tendencies toward a unified private law
  and, 103; terminology, 6–7
Civil law nations, 1
Civil law system, 6
Civil law tradition: comparative perspective on, 152; and critical attitudes
  toward legal science, 150–151; criticisms of, 148; is critically examined,
  149; is in constant transition, 149;
  modern changes in, 151–152; overview of, 2–5; perspectives on variety
  in, 146–147
Civil lawyers, 26
Civil procedure: appeal in, 123–124;
  damages and, 126; differences
  between civil law and common law

171

Index

Index

Law education, 68–69. *See also* Legal profession(s)
Law firms, 108
Lawmaking: judicial, 17, 85, 157; separation of powers and, 23; sovereignty and, 21–22; state positivism and, 23
Law professors, 110–112. *See also* Legal scholars
Lebanon, 4
Legal acts, 78, 79. *See also* Juridical acts
Legal acts in the strict sense, 78
Legal advisers, 108
Legal facts, 77–78
Legal history, 61
Legality, 129
Legal norm, 72–73, 77–78
Legal order, 71–73
Legal positivism, 21
Legal profession(s): academic lawyers, 110–111; advocates, 107–108; in America, 104; civil law-common law distinctions in the judiciary, 112–113; in the civil law world, 104–105; government lawyers, 107; judges, 105–106; notaries, 109–110; public prosecutors, 106–107
"Legal proof," 120–121
Legal realists, 69
Legal relation, 74–77
Legal scholars: discussion of, 57–62; expanding their field of study, 100; the legal process and, 82, 84, 86–87; resistance to change, 86–87
Legal science: the common law world and, 68–69, 81; concept and characteristics of, 64–67; consequences of defining and categorizing law, 93–94; critical attitudes toward, 150–151; European liberalism and, 67; expansion of the field of study in, 100; Germany and, 63–64; historical background of, 63; the legal process and, 84–85; liberalism and, 95
Legal systems, 1
Legal traditions, 1–5
Legislation: constitutional review, 137–144; formal and substantive validity, 141; as law, 24, 27; law of the general part and, 80–81; the legal process and, 83; "special," 155–158
Legislative decree, 159
Legislative positivism, 23–24
Legislative power, 23–24

Legislators: dogma of infallibility and, 57; the legal process and, 82–83
Legislature(s): decline in authority of, 158–159; dogma of infallibility and, 57; equitable power and, 52–53; power of, 23–24; statutory interpretation in France and, 40
Lenin, Vladimir, 97
Les grands arrêts, 91
Liberalism, 67, 95
Liberty: of the individual, 18
Licit acts, 78
Logic: legal science and, 66
Logical expansion, 66
"Logically formal rationalism," 66

Maine, Sir Henry, 18
Mandado de segurança, 55, 145
Mandamus, 17, 90
Marbury v. Madison, 142
Mexico: *amparo* procedure, 55; Constitution of 1917, 98; judicial review and, 25
Microsystems, 155–157, 158
Model fact situation, 73, 78
Montesquieu, 16, 17
Mos gallicus, 63
Mos italicus, 63
Mussolini, Benito, 48

Napoléon Bonaparte, 59, 60
Nationalism, 18–19
National law, 18–19
National legal systems, 1, 18–19, 21
Nation-states, 10, 21
Natural law: objective law and, 72; statutory interpretation and, 45. *See also* Roman Catholic Church, natural law; Secular natural law
Natural rights, 19
Nazi Germany, 54
Norms, 72. *See also* Legal norm
Notaries, 109–110
Notary public, 109
Nulla poena sine lege, 127
Nullum crimen sine lege, 127

Objective law, 72
Obligation, 76
Of Crimes and Punishments (Beccaria), 127–128
Operations, 78
Opinions: judicial, 124–125

9 781503 607545